WHAT'S FOR DINNER?

SALLY MANSFIELD
and the Family Circle Cookery Team

WHAT'S FOR DINNER?

SALLY MANSFIELD
and the Family Circle Cookery Team

NOTES

ALL RECIPES SERVE 4

ALL NUTRIENTS ARE APPROXIMATE

STANDARD LEVEL SPOON MEASUREMENTS ARE USED IN ALL RECIPES
1 TABLESPOON = ONE 15 ML SPOON
1 TEASPOON = ONE 5 ML SPOON

BOTH IMPERIAL AND METRIC MEASUREMENTS HAVE BEEN GIVEN IN ALL RECIPES
USE ONE SET OF MEASUREMENTS ONLY AND NOT A MIXTURE OF BOTH

SEASONING AND GARNISHES ARE NOT INCLUDED IN THE LISTS OF INGREDIENTS

EGGS SHOULD BE SIZE 3 UNLESS OTHERWISE STATED

MILK SHOULD BE SEMI-SKIMMED UNLESS OTHERWISE STATED

FRESH HERBS SHOULD BE USED UNLESS OTHERWISE STATED. IF UNAVAILABLE USE DRIED
HERBS AS AN ALTERNATIVE BUT HALVE THE QUANTITIES STATED

OVENS SHOULD BE PREHEATED TO THE SPECIFIED TEMPERATURE – IF USING A FAN ASSISTED OVEN
FOLLOW MANUFACTURER'S INSTRUCTIONS FOR ADJUSTING THE TIME AND THE TEMPERATURE

ALL MICROWAVE INFORMATION IS BASED ON A 650 WATT OVEN. FOLLOW MANUFACTURER'S
INSTRUCTIONS FOR AN OVEN WITH A DIFFERENT WATTAGE

NOTE FOR VEGETARIANS: PECORINO IS A VEGETARIAN SUBSTITUTE FOR PARMESAN

First published in Great Britain in 1994 by Hamlyn
an imprint of Reed Consumer Books Limited
Michelin House, 81 Fulham Road, London SW3 6RB
and Auckland, Melbourne, Singapore and Toronto

ISBN 0 600 582 353

A CIP catalogue record for this book is available from the British Library

Colour reproduction by Dot Gradations, Chelmsford, Essex

Produced by Mandarin Offset
Printed in Hong Kong

Acknowledgements

Editor: *Jo Lethaby*
Art Editor: *Meryl James*
Production Controller: *Sasha Judelson*
Design: *Town Group Consultancy Limited*

Family Circle Editor: *Gilly Batterbee*
Family Circle Practicals Editor: *Maggi Altham*
Family Circle Food and Drink Editor: *Sally Mansfield;* Deputy: *Matthew Drennan*
Senior Food and Drink Writer: *Lauren Floodgate*
Photographers: *Karl Adamson, Edward Alwright, Clint Brown, James Duncan, Dave Jordan,*
Michael Michaels, Ian O'Leary, Tony Robins, Simon Smith, Clive Streeter
Stylists: *Madeleine Brehaut, Suzy Gittins, Philomena Michaels, Felicity Salter, Judy Williams*

CONTENTS

INTRODUCTION

With the hectic pace of life today it's not surprising that many of us find ourselves racking our brains to come up with nourishing main meals that are going to suit the family's tastes – and then finding we have just 10 minutes flat to get the food cooked and on the table.

Because we know our readers find our regular What's for Dinner? feature a godsend, we've put together over 200 recipes published in *Family Circle* into this book. There are six chapters – from tasty and cheap to something just that little bit special – and every recipe is photographed to show how the food will look, with a breakdown of preparation and cooking times plus calorie, total fat, fibre and carbohydrate content for every serving.

Each recipe is calculated to serve a family of four but can be easily adapted to suit your particular needs.

Here's to happy cooking – and eating ...

Sally Mansfield

Food and Drink Editor, *Family Circle*

TASTY AND CHEAP

Chicken and vegetable risotto

- 2½ lb (1.1 kg) packet frozen chicken portions, thawed
- 1 tablespoon vegetable oil
- 1 onion, thinly sliced
- 8 oz (225 g) courgettes, thickly sliced
- 6 oz (150 g) long grain rice
- 1 pint (568 ml) chicken stock
- 7 oz (200 g) can red kidney beans, drained
- 2 tomatoes, peeled, deseeded and cut into strips
- 3 tablespoons grated parmesan

1. Remove skin and bones from each chicken portion and cut meat into bite-sized pieces.
2. Heat oil in a large frying pan and cook onion for 2-3 minutes until tender. Add chicken to the pan and cook for 5 minutes until meat is pale golden
3. Add sliced courgettes and cook for 2 minutes. Add rice and stir in chicken stock. Cover pan and cook over a low heat for a further 10-15 minutes or until rice is tender.
4. Add red kidney beans and tomato strips and continue to heat for another 5 minutes. Stir in grated parmesan and season well before serving.

TIME: *preparation 20 minutes; cooking 30 minutes*
NUTRIENTS PER SERVING: *Calories 405; Total fat 12 g; Fibre 5 g; Carbohydrate 44 g*

FOOD EDITOR'S TIP

The chicken portions may be cooked beforehand and added to the risotto towards the end.

Spicy chicken

- 4 frozen chicken breasts, thawed
- ½ x 9 fl oz (250 ml) bottle teriyaki marinade and sauce
- 2 tablespoons clear honey
- 4 oz (100 g) medium egg thread noodles
- 1 pint (568 ml) boiling water

1 Remove skin and bone from chicken. Mix together teriyaki marinade and honey in a shallow dish. Put in chicken breasts and spoon over marinade to coat. Cover and leave for 1 hour.
2 Remove chicken from dish, reserving marinade. Cook under a preheated grill for 10 minutes until golden, turning once.
3 Meanwhile, put noodles in a bowl and cover with boiling water. Leave to stand for 10 minutes until tender, or according to packet instructions. Drain.
4 Pour marinade into a small pan and bring to boil. Boil for 5 minutes until liquid is reduced by half and is syrupy. Slice each chicken breast into five pieces and arrange on serving plates. Drizzle over sauce. Serve with noodles, garnished with strips of spring onion, accompanied by mixed vegetables and any remaining marinade.

TIME: *preparation 25 minutes; marinating 1 hour; standing 10 minutes; cooking 15 minutes*
NUTRIENTS PER SERVING: *Calories 270; Total fat 7 g; Fibre 1 g; Carbohydrate 27 g*

FOOD EDITOR'S TIP

Slash chicken breasts a few times with a sharp knife before pouring over the marinade so the flavours can really penetrate.

Quick turkey curry and rice

- 4 tablespoons vegetable oil
- 1 lb (450 g) diced frozen turkey, thawed
- 8 oz (225 g) onions, thinly sliced
- 1 oz (25 g) plain flour
- 2 tablespoons medium madras curry powder
- 1 pint (568 ml) chicken stock
- 14 oz (397 g) can chopped tomatoes
- 12 oz (325 g) potatoes, roughly chopped
- 6 oz (150 g) carrots, roughly chopped
- 3 tablespoons mango chutney
- 2 oz (50 g) sultanas
- 4 oz (100 g) green apple, unpeeled, chopped
- 12 oz (325 g) basmati rice
- 1½ pints (852 ml) boiling water

1 Heat oil in a large frying pan and fry turkey for 5 minutes, stirring continuously until golden.
2 Add sliced onions and cook for 3 minutes until soft.
3 Stir in flour and curry powder and cook for 1 minute, stirring. Stir in chicken stock and chopped tomatoes. Bring to the boil, stirring until thickened.
4 Stir in potatoes, carrots, mango chutney and sultanas. Cover and simmer for 20 minutes. Uncover, stir in chopped apple and cook for a further 5 minutes.
5 Meanwhile, cook basmati rice in lightly salted boiling water for 10 minutes or according to packet instructions.
6 Spoon rice and curry on to hot serving plates. Garnish with fresh coriander and serve with poppadoms and cucumber raita.

TIME: *preparation 20 minutes; cooking 34 minutes*
NUTRIENTS PER SERVING: *Calories 750; Total fat 18 g; Fibre 6 g; Carbohydrate 112 g*

FOOD EDITOR'S TIP

Using basmati rice adds a nuttier flavour than long grain rice.

Turkey pie

- 9 oz (250 g) plain flour
- 5 oz (125 g) block margarine
- 2 tablespoons chopped fresh parsley
- 1 lb (450 g) frozen turkey pieces, thawed
- 5 fl oz (142 ml) milk
- 8 oz (225 g) button mushrooms
- 2 spring onions, trimmed and sliced

1 Sift 8 oz (225 g) plain flour into a large bowl. Rub in 4 oz (100 g) margarine until mixture resembles fine breadcrumbs.
2 Stir in parsley, seasoning and enough cold water to form a soft dough. Put in a polybag and chill for 30 minutes.
3 Meanwhile, put turkey pieces into a pan with milk. Simmer for 15 minutes or until turkey is tender. Drain milk and reserve.
4 Melt remaining margarine in a pan and fry mushrooms and onions for 5 minutes until just tender. Sprinkle in remaining flour and stir over a medium heat for 1 minute. Stir in reserved milk. Cook, stirring continuously, until mixture thickens. Season well, then add turkey.
5 Spoon turkey mixture into the base of an 8 inch (20.5 cm) pie plate. Roll out pastry on a lightly floured surface and cut into 1 inch (2.5 cm) wide strips. Arrange in an overlapping lattice pattern on top of filling. Trim edges.
6 Re-roll trimmings, cut out leaves. Dampen and arrange around edge of pie. Brush pie with beaten egg or milk and cook at 400°F (200°C), Gas 6 for 35-40 minutes. Serve with baked potatoes and mixed vegetables.

TIME: *preparation 45 minutes; chilling 30 minutes; cooking 1 hour 1 minute*
NUTRIENTS PER SERVING: *Calories 580; Total fat 29 g; Fibre 3 g; Carbohydrate 51 g*

FOOD EDITOR'S TIP

Turkey drumsticks can be used, removing the bones after step 3.

Chilli beef and pasta

- 1 tablespoon vegetable oil
- 1 large onion, finely chopped
- 1 garlic clove, crushed
- 1 lb (450 g) minced beef
- 1 tablespoon mild chilli powder
- 1 tablespoon tomato purée
- 14 oz (397 g) can chopped tomatoes with herbs
- 7 oz (200 g) can red kidney beans, drained
- 10 fl oz (284 ml) beef stock
- 4 oz (100 g) pasta twists
- ½ white cob loaf
- 2 oz (50 g) butter
- 1 teaspoon dried mixed herbs

1 Heat oil in a large saucepan. Fry chopped onion and crushed garlic for about 3-4 minutes. Add minced beef and cook, stirring occasionally, until meat has browned.
2 Stir in chilli powder and tomato purée. Cook for 1-2 minutes. Add chopped tomatoes, drained kidney beans, beef stock and pasta twists and season well.
3 Gently simmer mixture over a low heat for 20 minutes, stirring occasionally.
4 Meanwhile, split half of a cob loaf through the middle. Spread one side with butter and sprinkle with herbs. Sandwich together. Cut into four wedges.
5 Wrap bread wedges together in foil and cook at 325°F (160°C), Gas 3 for 15 minutes to heat through.
6 Spoon chilli and pasta into individual serving bowls and garnish with a little chopped fresh parsley. Serve immediately with the hot, buttery herb bread.

TIME: *preparation 20 minutes; cooking 26 minutes*
NUTRIENTS PER SERVING: *Calories 530; Total fat 21 g; Fibre 5 g; Carbohydrate 56 g*

FOOD EDITOR'S TIP

If using fresh mixed herbs, increase to 1 tablespoon.

Moussaka aubergines

- 2 medium aubergines, halved
- 1 lb (450 g) lean minced beef
- 1 onion, chopped
- 2 garlic cloves, crushed
- 14 oz (397 g) can tomatoes
- 2 tablespoons tomato purée
- 2 teaspoons salt
- 1 oz (25 g) butter
- 1 oz (25 g) plain flour
- 10 fl oz (284 ml) semi-skimmed milk
- 4 oz (100 g) cheddar, grated
- 1 oz (25 g) Granary breadcrumbs

1 Scoop out aubergine flesh and dice.
2 Dry-fry beef, onion and garlic for 12 minutes. Add aubergine, tomatoes and purée.
3 Cover, simmer for 45 minutes, stirring occasionally. Cook, uncovered, for 30 minutes.
4 Meanwhile, salt aubergine shells for 30 minutes. Rinse and cook in boiling water for 5 minutes. Drain and pat dry. Spoon in filling.
5 Melt butter, add flour, cook 1 minute. Add milk, cook until thickened. Stir in half the cheese, season.
6 Top filling with sauce, crumbs and remaining cheese. Grill 2 minutes. Serve with baked potatoes and salad. Garnish with chopped parsley.

TIME: *preparation 30 minutes; cooking 1 hour 29 minutes*
NUTRIENTS PER SERVING: *Calories 410; Total fat 21 g; Fibre 4 g; Carbohydrate 20 g*

FOOD EDITOR'S TIP

Use a grapefruit knife to cut out the aubergine flesh.

Cheesy all-in-one burgers

- 1 lb (450 g) lean minced beef
- 4 oz (100 g) onion, finely chopped
- 1 garlic clove, crushed
- 10.2 oz (290 g) packet pizza base mix
- 4 slices processed cheese
- 1 egg (size 3), beaten
- 1 tablespoon poppy seeds

1 Mix mince, onion and garlic together. Season well. Divide into quarters and shape into four 4 inch (10 cm) burgers. Put on a greased baking sheet, chill for 10 minutes.
2   Meanwhile, make up pizza base mix according to packet instructions. Knead for 5 minutes. Divide into four and roll each piece out to an 8 inch (20 cm) circle.
3 Put cheese slice and burger in middle of each circle. Brush edges with egg, wrap around burgers. Seal and put seam-side down on baking sheet. Leave to rise for 10 minutes.
4 Brush top of dough with egg and sprinkle over poppy seeds. Cook at 350°F (180°C), Gas 4 for 30 minutes, until golden brown.
5 Serve with onion rings, sautéd potatoes and peas.

TIME: *preparation 20 minutes; chilling 10 minutes; proving 10 minutes; cooking 30 minutes*
NUTRIENTS PER SERVING: *Calories 520; Total fat 19 g; Fibre Trace; Carbohydrate 52 g*

FOOD EDITOR'S TIP

If the kids want a bit more 'bite', add a dash of cucumber and tomato relish to the burgers.

Toad-in-the-hole

- 4 oz (100 g) plain flour
- 1 egg (size 3)
- 10 fl oz (284 ml) milk
- 1 tablespoon vegetable oil
- 1 onion, thinly sliced
- 1 lb (450 g) pork and beef sausages
- 2 tomatoes, quartered

1 Sift plain flour and a little seasoning into a bowl. Add egg with the milk and mix to a smooth batter.
2 Heat oil in a frying pan and gently fry onion for about 2-3 minutes until tender. Add pork and beef sausages and fry them for 4-5 minutes until browned. Put sausages and onion in a preheated well-greased 3 pint (1.7 litre) ovenproof dish.
3 Add tomato quarters and pour in the batter. Cook at 425°F (220°C), Gas 7 for 30 minutes, until the batter is well risen and golden brown.
4 Serve with garlic potatoes and vegetables.

TIME: *preparation 20 minutes; cooking 38 minutes*
NUTRIENTS PER SERVING: *Calories 590; Total fat 41 g; Fibre 2 g; Carbohydrate 39 g*

FOOD EDITOR'S TIP

You can change the flavour of the batter by adding 1 tablespoon fresh chopped herbs or 2 oz (50 g) chopped mushrooms.

Spicy pasta bake

- 1 lb (450 g) lean minced beef
- 4 oz (100 g) onion, finely chopped
- 1 garlic clove, crushed
- ½ red pepper, sliced
- 4 oz (100 g) button mushrooms, sliced
- 14 oz (397 g) can chopped tomatoes
- few drops Tabasco sauce
- ½ teaspoon cinnamon
- 8 oz (225 g) penne pasta
- 10 oz (275 g) natural yogurt
- 1 egg (size 3), beaten
- 1 tablespoon cornflour
- 2 oz (50 g) cheddar, grated

1 Mix mince, onion and garlic together. Season well. Dry-fry in a large nonstick pan for 5 minutes until browned, stirring occasionally.
2 Add red pepper and mushrooms. Cook for 5 minutes until soft.
3 Stir in tomatoes, Tabasco and cinnamon. Season and simmer for 10 minutes, stirring occasionally.
4 Meanwhile, cook pasta in plenty of salted boiling water for 12 minutes or according to packet instructions. Drain.
5 Spoon pasta into base of an oiled 3 pint (1.7 litre) shallow ovenproof dish. Top with mince.
6 Beat together yogurt, egg and cornflour until smooth. Season well. Pour over mince and sprinkle with grated cheese. Cook at 350°F (180°C), Gas 4 for 40 minutes or until golden brown.
7 Serve with mixed salad leaves.

TIME: *preparation 15 minutes; cooking 1 hour*
NUTRIENTS PER SERVING: *Calories 530; Total fat 15 g; Fibre 7 g; Carbohydrate 59 g*

FOOD EDITOR'S TIP

Tabasco sauce adds a bit of spice to any minced beef recipe.

Sausage spirals and ratatouille

- 2 leeks, sliced
- 1 packet mixed red, yellow and green peppers, deseeded and diced
- 1 garlic clove, crushed
- 3 tablespoons olive oil
- 14 oz (397 g) can tomatoes
- 3 tablespoons tomato purée
- pinch of sugar
- 1 bay leaf
- 4 sprigs fresh thyme, or ½ teaspoon dried
- 2 x 1 lb (450 g) packs cumberland sausages

1   Fry leeks, peppers and garlic in 1 tablespoon olive oil for 5 minutes. Add tomatoes, purée, sugar, bay leaf, thyme and seasoning.
2   Bring mixture to boil. Simmer uncovered, stirring for 30 minutes until vegetables are soft.
3   Meanwhile, carefully untwist sausages at the joins and squeeze sausagemeat into gaps to form two long, continuous sausages.
4   Halve each long sausage, coil and secure with cocktail sticks. Heat remaining oil, fry in batches of two for 5 minutes each side.
5   Serve Sausage Spirals and Ratatouille with baked potato and mustard. Garnish with chives and thyme.

TIME: *preparation 15 minutes; cooking 35 minutes*
NUTRIENTS PER SERVING: *Calories 540; Total fat 41 g; Fibre 3 g; Carbohydrate 23 g*

FOOD EDITOR'S TIP

Make sure you coil up the sausages starting at the cut end.

Sausage slice

- 1 onion, chopped
- 8.1 oz (230 g) can chopped tomatoes
- 2 tablespoons tomato purée
- ½ teaspoon dried mixed herbs
- 3 eggs (size 3)
- 1 lb (450 g) premium sausagemeat
- 1 lb 2 oz (500 g) packet frozen puff pastry, thawed

1   Put onion, chopped tomatoes, tomato purée and herbs into a small saucepan and cook over a low heat for 15 minutes, until thick and reduced by half.
2   Meanwhile, boil 2 eggs for 10 minutes, shell and chop. Set aside. Season sausagemeat. Cut pastry in half. Roll out half to make a 10 x 6 inch (25.5 x 15 cm) rectangle and the remainder to a 12 x 7 inch (30.5 x 18 cm) rectangle on a surface lightly dusted with flour.
3   Transfer smaller sheet of pastry on to a greased baking sheet. Spread tomato sauce down centre of pastry. Top with chopped egg. Put sausagemeat down centre. Put remaining pastry on top. Seal edges with a little beaten egg, glaze with remaining egg.
4   Cook at 400°F (200°C), Gas 6 for 40 minutes. Serve with mushrooms and broccoli.

TIME: *preparation 15 minutes; cooking 55 minutes*
NUTRIENTS PER SERVING: *Calories 770; Total fat 51 g; Fibre 1 g; Carbohydrate 53 g*

FOOD EDITOR'S TIP

This is just as delicious served cold and makes a great lunch box filler.

Country patties

- 8 oz (225 g) pig's liver, sliced
- 1 lb (450 g) belly pork, diced
- 1 onion, sliced
- 2 tablespoons dried sage
- 1 garlic clove, crushed
- 2 tablespoons chopped fresh parsley
- 4 oz (100 g) white breadcrumbs
- 2 eggs (size 3), beaten
- 1 tablespoon cornflour
- ½ teaspoon English mustard powder
- 10 fl oz (284 ml) warm beef stock

1 Put liver, pork, onion, sage and garlic into a pan, and cook for 40 minutes. Drain well.
2 Process in a liquidizer or food processor in three batches. Spoon into a bowl. Stir in parsley, breadcrumbs, eggs and seasoning.
3 Divide mixture into twelve, shape into ovals. Put in one layer in a greased roasting tin.
4 Cover with greased foil, cook at 350°F (180°C), Gas 4 for 30 minutes. Remove foil, cook for 15 minutes.
5 Mix cornflour, mustard and a little stock. Pour into a pan with remaining stock. Stir over a medium heat until thickened. Serve with broccoli, carrots, green beans, cauliflower and potatoes.

TIME: *preparation 30 minutes; cooking 1 hour 25 minutes*
NUTRIENTS PER SERVING: *Calories 510; Total fat 33 g; Fibre 1 g; Carbohydrate 19 g*

FOOD EDITOR'S TIP

If you can't get belly pork use boned shoulder instead.

Spinach rolls

- 5 oz (125 g) plain flour
- 5 oz (125 g) plain wholemeal flour
- 2½ oz (65 g) white vegetable fat, cubed
- 2½ oz (65 g) butter, cubed
- 5 tablespoons iced water
- 8 oz (225 g) frozen chopped spinach
- ½ red pepper, deseeded and diced
- 1 onion, finely chopped
- 1 tablespoon chopped fresh parsley
- ½ tablespoon chopped fresh rosemary
- 8 oz (225 g) pork sausagemeat
- 1 egg (size 3), beaten

1 Rub flours and fats together until mixture resembles fine breadcrumbs. Stir in enough iced water to form a smooth, soft dough. Wrap and chill for 10 minutes.
2 Cook spinach in a pan over a low heat, stirring until all liquid has evaporated. Cool.
3 Mix together red pepper, onion, parsley, rosemary and sausagemeat. Season well.
4 Roll out chilled pastry on a lightly floured surface to an 11 x 10 inch (28 x 25 cm) rectangle. Cut in half lengthways.
5 Divide sausage mixture in half and roll into two 11 inch (28 cm) sausages. Lay one sausage along centre of each pastry rectangle. Divide spinach in half and spread over each roll. Roll up carefully and seal with a little beaten egg.
6 Cut each roll in half and put on a baking sheet. Make diagonal cuts in top and brush with egg. Cook at 400°F (200°C), Gas 6 for 25 minutes. Garnish with rosemary. Serve with pan-fried aubergines and a mixed bean salad.

TIME: *preparation 25 minutes; chilling 10 minutes; cooking 25 minutes*
NUTRIENTS PER SERVING: *Calories 700; Total fat 47 g; Fibre 14 g; Carbohydrate 53 g*

FOOD EDITOR'S TIP

For a quicker dish look out for chilled ready-made wholemeal pastry.

Sweet and sour pork

- 1 lb (450 g) frozen diced pork, thawed
- 2 oz (50 g) plain flour
- 1 tablespoon cornflour
- 1 egg (size 3), white only
- groundnut oil, for frying
- 9 oz (240 g) packet prepared stir-fry vegetables
- 2 oz (50 g) packet sweet and sour sauce mix

1 Trim excess fat from pork. Put 2 tablespoons flour into a polybag, add pork and shake to coat. Put remaining flour into a bowl.
2 Add cornflour and egg white to bowl, and stir in enough cold water to form a smooth batter, the consistency of single cream.
3 Heat oil in a deep pan until a cube of bread rises and sizzles within 30 seconds. Dip pork, six pieces at a time into batter then fry in oil in four batches for 5 minutes each until set and pale golden. Drain pork on kitchen paper and keep warm.
4 Meanwhile, heat 2 teaspoons oil in a wok or frying pan and stir-fry vegetables for 3-4 minutes until tender.
5 Mix sweet and sour sauce mix with 6 fl oz (170 ml) water, or as directed on packet, and stir over a medium heat until smooth and thickened slightly.
6 Spoon pork on to serving plates with stir-fried vegetables. Spoon a little sweet and sour sauce over each portion. Serve with egg noodles garnished with parsley, and prawn crackers.

TIME: *preparation 30 minutes; cooking 20 minutes*
NUTRIENTS PER SERVING: *Calories 380; Total fat 24 g; Fibre 1 g; Carbohydrate 14 g*

FOOD EDITOR'S TIP

Add pork to oil one piece at a time with tongs, to help prevent sticking.

Cheesy broccoli bake

- 4 oz (100 g) macaroni
- 1 lb (450 g) cauliflower florets
- 1 lb (450 g) broccoli florets
- 2 oz (50 g) low-fat spread
- 2 oz (50 g) plain flour
- 1 pint (568 ml) skimmed milk
- ½ teaspoon English mustard
- 6 oz (150 g) reduced-fat cheddar, grated

1 Cook macaroni according to packet instructions. Meanwhile, cook cauliflower and broccoli in plenty of salted boiling water for 4 minutes, until just tender. Drain and reserve.
2 Melt low-fat spread in a saucepan. Stir in plain flour and cook for 1 minute, stirring. Gradually add milk and bring to boil, stirring until thickened.
3 Remove from heat, season and stir in mustard and 3 oz (75 g) grated cheese.
4 Stir macaroni, cauliflower and broccoli into cheese sauce. Spoon mixture into four 10 fl oz (284 ml) ovenproof dishes.
5 Sprinkle remaining cheese over and cook at 400°F (200°C), Gas 6 for 25 minutes until golden.
6 Serve with spinach and a bacon salad.

TIME: *preparation 20 minutes; cooking 30 minutes*
NUTRIENTS PER SERVING: *Calories 400; Total fat 13 g; Fibre 6 g; Carbohydrate 41 g*

FOOD EDITOR'S TIP

If broccoli is unavailable use 2 lb (900 g) cauliflower florets and add 2 tablespoons chopped fresh parsley for colour.

Boston beans and bread

- 2 tablespoons vegetable oil
- 1 onion, finely sliced
- 3 teaspoons garlic purée
- 2 x 15¼ oz (432 g) cans red kidney beans, rinsed and drained
- 15¼ oz (432 g) can soya beans, rinsed and drained
- 3 tablespoons Worcestershire sauce
- 3 tablespoons tomato purée
- 2 oz (50 g) molasses
- 2 oz (50 g) light brown soft sugar
- 1 tablespoon dried English mustard
- 10 fl oz (284 ml) vegetable stock
- 3 fresh bay leaves
- 8 oz (225 g) unsmoked bacon joint, shredded
- 1 small wholemeal baguette
- 1 tablespoon chopped fresh parsley
- 2 oz (50 g) butter, softened

1 Heat oil in a large saucepan, add onion and cook for 2 minutes until tender. Stir in 1 teaspoon of the garlic purée and cook for 30 seconds.
2 Add all the beans, Worcestershire sauce, tomato purée, molasses, sugar, English mustard and stock. Stir over a low heat until the molasses and sugar have dissolved.
3 Stir in bay leaves and bacon. Season and simmer for 40 minutes.
4 Meanwhile, make eleven diagonal cuts in baguette. Mix remaining 2 teaspoons garlic purée and parsley with softened butter. Spread between slices. Wrap in foil, bake at 400°F (200°C), Gas 6 for 30 minutes.
5 Serve Boston Beans with the hot garlic bread.

TIME: *preparation 15 minutes; cooking 48 minutes*
NUTRIENTS PER SERVING: *Calories 700; Total fat 28 g; Fibre 16 g; Carbohydrate 80 g*

FOOD EDITOR'S TIP

This is an ideal way of cooking cheaper cuts of bacon.

Pan haggerty

- 3 tablespoons vegetable oil
- 2 lb (900 g) potatoes, thinly sliced
- 2 medium onions, thinly sliced
- ½ teaspoon ground nutmeg
- 8 oz (225 g) rindless bacon, grilled and shredded
- 3 tomatoes, thinly sliced
- 2 oz (50 g) wholemeal breadcrumbs
- 2 tablespoons snipped fresh chives

1 Heat oil in a large nonstick frying pan. Arrange half the potatoes over base, then layer onions, nutmeg and bacon on top. Season well. Cover with remaining potato slices.
2 Cover and cook over a low heat for 30 minutes.
3 Lay tomato slices across potato in lines about 1 inch (2.5 cm) apart. Sprinkle breadcrumbs inbetween. Grill for 4 minutes, until breadcrumbs are golden brown.
4 Spoon on to plates, sprinkle over chives and serve with salad.

TIME: *preparation 15 minutes; cooking 34 minutes*
NUTRIENTS PER SERVING: *Calories 600; Total fat 34 g; Fibre 6 g; Carbohydrate 58 g*

FOOD EDITOR'S TIP

Make sure the potatoes are very thinly sliced. Your processor or grater may have a slicing facility.

Spinach and bacon

- 1 lb (450 g) frozen chopped spinach, defrosted
- 4½ oz (115 g) parmesan, grated
- 3 eggs (size 3), beaten
- 1 garlic clove, crushed
- 2 rashers streaky bacon, grilled and finely chopped

1 Cook chopped spinach in a large saucepan over a low heat for 10 minutes, stirring frequently until all of the excess liquid has evaporated.

2 Transfer spinach to a bowl and stir in all but 1 tablespoon of grated parmesan along with eggs and crushed garlic.

3 Spoon mixture into a greased 7 inch (18 cm) round sandwich tin, levelling surface with the back of a spoon. Cook at 375°F (190°C), Gas 5 for 30 minutes or until mixture is set.

4 Sprinkle spinach bake with grilled bacon pieces and reserved parmesan. Serve cut into wedges and garnished with sliced tomatoes, onions and oakleaf lettuce.

TIME: *preparation 15 minutes; cooking 40 minutes*
NUTRIENTS PER SERVING: *Calories 280; Total fat 20; Fibre 2 g; Carbohydrate trace*

FOOD EDITOR'S TIP

To make this a vegetarian dish, use fried mushrooms sprinkled on top instead of bacon.

Bacon steaks and rosti

- 1½ lb (675 g) potatoes, peeled
- 8 bacon steaks
- 2 tablespoons wholegrain mustard
- 2 oz (50 g) plain flour
- 2 eggs (size 3), beaten
- ½ white cob loaf, made into breadcrumbs
- 8 tablespoons vegetable oil
- 1 onion, grated

1 Boil potatoes for 15 minutes until tender. Leave until cold, then coarsely grate.

2 Meanwhile, trim fat from bacon. Spread one side of steaks with mustard.

3 Dip each steak into flour, then egg and coat in breadcrumbs.

4 Heat a little vegetable oil. Fry steaks for 5 minutes each side until golden. Drain.

5 Mix together potato, onion and seasoning. Heat remaining oil in a pan. Add potato mixture.

6 Flatten mixture over base of pan and cook for 5 minutes. Invert on to plate, return to pan and cook for a further 5 minutes until golden.

7 Serve the Bacon Steaks and Rosti, cut into wedges, with savoy cabbage.

TIME: *preparation 30 minutes; cooking 35 minutes*
NUTRIENTS PER SERVING: *Calories 750; Total fat 37 g; Fibre 4 g; Carbohydrate 61 g*

Golden eggs

- 2 tablespoons white wine vinegar
- 1 bay leaf
- 6 eggs (size 3)
- 6 oz (150 g) butter, melted
- 4 x 3 oz (75 g) gammon steaks
- 2 x 8 oz (227 g) packets 4 potato waffles
- 1 lb (450 g) tomatoes

1 To make hollandaise sauce: heat vinegar, bay leaf and 1 tablespoon water and reduce to 1 tablespoon of liquid. Remove bay leaf.
2 Blend in a food processor with 2 egg yolks. With machine on full speed, gradually pour in melted butter until thickened.
3 Grill gammon steaks and potato waffles for 10 minutes.
4 Halve tomatoes. After first 5 minutes, add to grill. Cook for a further 5 minutes, turning once.
5 Meanwhile, grease four poaching cups. Half fill the pan with boiling water. Crack an egg into each cup, place in pan and cover. Cook for 5-6 minutes.
6 Pour hollandaise sauce into a pan and warm over a low heat.
7 Put two waffles on each plate, top with bacon and an egg. Spoon sauce over. Serve with tomatoes and salad, garnish with parsley.

TIME: *preparation 25 minutes; cooking 16 minutes*
NUTRIENTS PER SERVING: *Calories 690; Total fat 49 g; Fibre 2 g; Carbohydrate 34 g*

FOOD EDITOR'S TIP

If you don't have an egg poacher, cook the eggs in four greased tea cups standing in a pan of water.

Multi-mix fried rice

- 15¼ oz (432 g) can pineapple slices in syrup, drained and syrup reserved
- 3 tablespoons distilled malt vinegar
- 1 tablespoon soy sauce
- 2 oz (50 g) demerara sugar
- 1 tablespoon tomato purée
- 2 tablespoons cornflour
- 3 tablespoons vegetable oil
- 10 oz (275 g) packet gammon steaks, shredded
- 1 packet mixed red, yellow and green peppers
- 1 bunch spring onions, roughly chopped
- 1 garlic clove, crushed
- 12 oz (325 g) basmati rice
- 4 oz (100 g) button mushrooms, sliced

1 Heat pineapple syrup, vinegar, soy sauce, sugar and tomato purée in a pan until sugar dissolves.
2 Mix cornflour with 2 tablespoons cold water to form a smooth paste. Pour into sauce and bring to boil, stirring. Remove from heat.
3 Heat oil in a frying pan. Stir-fry bacon for 5 minutes until golden. Thinly slice half red pepper and roughly chop other peppers. Stir peppers into bacon with spring onions and garlic. Stir-fry for 5 minutes.
4 Meanwhile, cook basmati rice in salted boiling water for 10 minutes or according to packet instructions.
5 Chop pineapple slices and stir into frying pan with mushrooms and rice. Stir-fry for 5 minutes. Meanwhile, gently re-heat sauce.
6 Spoon rice mixture on to plates and serve with sauce.

TIME: *preparation 15 minutes; cooking 25 minutes*
NUTRIENTS PER SERVING: *Calories 670; Total fat 17 g; Fibre 2 g; Carbohydrate 110 g*

FOOD EDITOR'S TIP

Any leftover cooked vegetables could be used in this recipe.

Cheesy bacon pies

- 1 lb (450 g) plain flour, sifted
- ¼ teaspoon salt
- ¼ teaspoon English mustard powder
- 8 oz (225 g) block margarine
- 4 oz (100 g) button mushrooms, sliced
- 8 oz (225 g) packet smoked bacon pieces
- 1 oz (25 g) butter
- 4 spring onions, sliced
- 1½ oz (40 g) walnut pieces
- 4 oz (100 g) blue stilton, cubed
- 1 egg (size 3), beaten

1. Mix together flour, salt and mustard powder. Rub in margarine and stir in enough water to form a soft dough. Chill.
2. Fry mushrooms and bacon in butter for 5 minutes. Add spring onions and cook for 2-3 minutes until soft. Spoon into a bowl, leave to cool.
3. Roll out pastry on a floured surface and using a 6½ inch (16.3 cm) plate as a guide, cut out six rounds. Re-roll trimmings and cut out two more rounds. Reserve remaining trimmings. Dampen edge of each round with water.
4. Add walnuts and stilton to mushroom mixture and season. Divide filling between pastry rounds. Bring edge of each round together above filling and press lightly to seal.
5. Roll out pastry trimmings and cut out 24 leaves. Using a pastry wheel, cut out 24 x 2½ inch (6.5 cm) fluted strips. Dampen and fix three leaves and three strips to each pie.
6. Arrange pies on two baking sheets, brush with beaten egg. Cook at 400°F (200°C), Gas 6 for 25 minutes. Serve with rolls, pickle and salad.

TIME: *preparation 40 minutes; cooking 33 minutes*
NUTRIENTS PER SERVING: *Calories 1,200; Total fat 84 g; Fibre 4 g; Carbohydrate 88 g*

FOOD EDITOR'S TIP

To seal the pastry properly, dampen the edges of each round very lightly with water.

Ham and leek flan

- 1 oz (25 g) parmesan, grated
- 8 oz (225 g) frozen shortcrust pastry, thawed
- 8 oz (225 g) leeks, thinly sliced
- 2 oz (50 g) butter
- 2 oz (50 g) plain flour
- 1 pint (568 ml) milk
- 2 eggs (size 3), beaten
- 2 oz (50 g) wafer-thin smoked ham, sliced

1. Lightly knead parmesan into pastry. Roll out on a surface lightly dusted with extra parmesan to make a circle large enough to line a deep 8 inch (20.5 cm) flan ring. Chill for 10 minutes.
2. Prick base and bake blind at 400°F (200°C), Gas 6 for 10 minutes. Remove baking beans and cook for a further 5 minutes.
3. Meanwhile, dry-fry leeks in a nonstick frying pan for 3 minutes. Melt butter in a small saucepan. Stir in plain flour and cook for 1 minute, stirring continuously. Gradually add milk, bring to boil, stirring until thickened.
4. Whisk together white sauce and eggs until smooth. Season well. Fold together leeks, sauce and ham. Spoon into cooked flan case. Cook at 375°F (190°C), Gas 5 for 50-55 minutes until golden. Serve with chips, carrots and peas. Garnish with parsley and piccalilli.

TIME: *preparation 20 minutes; chilling 10 minutes; cooking 1 hour 5 minutes*
NUTRIENTS PER SERVING: *Calories 520; Total fat 33 g; Fibre 3 g; Carbohydrate 42 g*

FOOD EDITOR'S TIP

Make sure pastry is thoroughly thawed and pliable before you knead with the parmesan.

Lancashire hotpots

- 2 lb (900 g) frozen stewing lamb, thawed
- 1 tablespoon vegetable oil
- 1 onion, sliced
- 2 tablespoons plain flour
- 1 tablespoon Worcestershire sauce
- 15 fl oz (426 ml) beef stock
- 4 sprigs fresh thyme, or ¼ teaspoon dried
- 2 lb (900 g) potatoes
- 1 oz (25 g) butter

1 Trim lamb. Fry meat in oil in two batches for 5 minutes each. Remove lamb, discard excess oil.
2 Fry onion for 5 minutes. Stir in flour and cook for 1 minute. Add Worcestershire sauce and stock. Cook, stirring, until thickened slightly.
3 Put meat and thyme into four 10fl oz (284 ml) ovenproof dishes. Pour onion gravy into each. Cut potatoes into thin slices. Arrange, overlapping, in two layers on top of meat.
4 Cover dishes with foil and put in a roasting tin. Cook at 350°F (180°C), Gas 4 for 1¼ hours. Remove foil, dot potatoes with butter. Cook for 30 minutes. Serve with peas and baby carrots.

TIME: *preparation 25 minutes; cooking 2 hours 1 minute*
NUTRIENTS PER SERVING: *Calories 550; Total fat 21 g; Fibre 3 g; Carbohydrate 45 g*

FOOD EDITOR'S TIP

Replace half the stock with stout to enhance the flavour.

Lamb and lentil curry

- 2 lb (900 g) bag diced frozen stewing lamb, thawed
- 10 oz (283 g) can mild korma curry sauce
- 4 oz (100 g) red lentils
- 1 teaspoon ground ginger
- 1 teaspoon ground turmeric
- 2 onions, peeled and sliced
- 2 garlic cloves, crushed
- 2 tablespoons vegetable oil

1 Put lamb into a shallow dish and cover with curry sauce. Leave to marinate.
2 Meanwhile, put lentils into a saucepan, cover with cold water and add ginger and turmeric. Bring lentils to boil, cover and simmer for 30 minutes, stirring occasionally, until soft and all water is absorbed.
3 Fry onions and garlic in oil for 5 minutes until golden. Stir in lamb mixture and lentils. Bring to boil, cover and simmer, stirring occasionally, for 45 minutes or until lamb is tender.
4 Garnish with tomato and fresh coriander. Serve with pilau rice and cucumber raita.

TIME: *preparation 15 minutes; cooking 1 hour 20 minutes*
NUTRIENTS PER SERVING: *Calories 530; Total fat 26 g; Fibre 4 g; Carbohydrate 26 g*

FOOD EDITOR'S TIP

For a richer flavour, leave the lamb to marinate in the curry sauce overnight.

Saucy fish pie

- 3 oz (75 g) butter
- 2 oz (50 g) plain flour
- 1¼ pints (710 ml) fish stock
- 14.1 oz (400 g) can tuna chunks in oil, drained
- 4 eggs (size 3), hard-boiled, shelled and quartered
- 1 lb (450 g) cooked potatoes

1 Melt 2 oz (50 g) butter in a heavy-based saucepan. Stir in flour and cook over a low heat for 1-2 minutes. Gradually add fish stock. Stirring continuously, cook over a low heat for a further 5 minutes until the sauce is smooth and thickened.
2 Carefully add chunks of tuna and quartered hard-boiled eggs to the sauce.
3 Spoon fish mixture into a 3 pint (1.7 litre) ovenproof dish. Slice cooked potatoes thickly and arrange on top. Melt remaining butter and brush over potatoes. Cook at 350°F (180°C), Gas 4 for 25 minutes, until the topping is golden brown.
4 Serve pie with sautéd onions and peas.

TIME: *preparation 20 minutes; cooking 32 minutes*
NUTRIENTS PER SERVING: *Calories 600; Total fat 41 g; Fibre 2 g; Carbohydrate 29 g*

FOOD EDITOR'S TIP

For an alternative try adding some cooked vegetables with the tuna in the sauce and as a good way of using up leftovers.

Paprika liver

- 1 lb (450 g) sliced lambs' liver
- 1 tablespoon plain flour
- 1 teaspoon paprika
- 4 medium onions, peeled and quartered
- 2 tablespoons vegetable oil
- 10 fl oz (284 ml) vegetable stock
- 2 tablespoons tomato purée
- ¼ teaspoon dried herbes de Provence

1 Cut liver into small slices. Rinse and pat dry with kitchen paper. Put flour, paprika and seasoning into a polybag. Add liver and shake well to coat.
2 Fry onions in oil for 5 minutes until golden. Remove with a slotted spoon. Add liver and fry for 4-5 minutes until just browned. Remove liver and keep hot.
3 Add stock, tomato purée and herbs to pan. Stir over a medium heat for 5 minutes until thickened and boiling. Return onions and liver to pan. Heat through for 3 minutes. Serve with mushroom savoury rice.

TIME: *preparation 15 minutes; cooking 18 minutes*
NUTRIENTS PER SERVING: *Calories 310; Total fat 18 g; Fibre 2 g; Carbohydrate 12 g*

FOOD EDITOR'S TIP

If you can't find any herbes de Provence try a mixture of dried thyme and parsley.

Smoked kedgeree

- 8 oz (225 g) easy-cook long grain rice
- 2 oz (50 g) frozen peas
- 8 oz (225 g) peppered mackerel fillets
- 2 eggs (size 3), hard-boiled, shelled and sliced
- 2 oz (50 g) butter, diced
- 3 tablespoons chopped fresh parsley

1 Put rice into a pan with a pinch of salt and 10 fl oz (284 ml) water. Bring to boil and simmer for 5 minutes.
2 Add peas to pan and cook for 5 minutes or until rice is tender. Drain well.
3 Meanwhile, flake fish, removing any bones. Put into pan with rice and heat gently for 5 minutes. Add sliced eggs to pan.
4 Add butter to pan and heat until melted. Toss pan contents lightly to coat with butter. Season and stir in parsley.
5 Spoon kedgeree on to serving plates, and garnish with sliced cherry tomatoes and fresh dill. Serve with crusty bread and lemon wedges to squeeze over.

TIME: *preparation 10 minutes; cooking 15 minutes*
NUTRIENTS PER SERVING: *Calories 490; Total fat 25 g; Fibre 1 g; Carbohydrate 49 g*

FOOD EDITOR'S TIP

You can use a mixture of long grain and wild rice for a 'nuttier' flavour.

Tuna and bean parcels

- 6 tablespoons sunflower oil
- 1 onion, chopped
- 1 garlic clove, crushed
- 8.1 oz (230 g) can chopped tomatoes
- 1 teaspoon tomato purée
- 6½ oz (185 g) can tuna chunks in brine, drained
- 7½ oz (213 g) can red kidney beans, rinsed and drained
- ½ x 7 oz (200 g) can cannellini beans, rinsed and drained
- 8 sheets filo pastry
- 8 oz (200 g) carton fromage frais
- 1 teaspoon chilli sauce

1 Heat 2 tablespoons oil in a frying pan, add onion and garlic. Cook for 2-3 minutes until soft. Stir in chopped tomatoes and tomato purée. Simmer for 10 minutes.
2 Stir in tuna, kidney beans and cannellini beans. Cook for a further 10 minutes. Leave to cool.
3 Cut the filo pastry sheets in half lengthways. Brush one strip of pastry lightly with a little of remaining oil and lay another piece on top.
4 Put 3-4 tablespoons of the tuna mixture at one end of the pastry. Fold over the sides and roll up. Put on a baking sheet and brush with oil. Repeat, using remaining pastry and filling until you have eight pastry parcels.
5 Cook parcels at 375°F (190°C), Gas 5 for 30 minutes or until golden.
6 Meanwhile, mix together fromage frais and chilli sauce. Serve Tuna and Bean Parcels with a mixed leaf salad.

TIME: *preparation 20 minutes; cooking 53 minutes*
NUTRIENTS PER SERVING: *Calories 490; Total fat 25 g; Fibre 5 g; Carbohydrate 46 g*

FOOD EDITOR'S TIP

Made into smaller parcels, these can be served at a dinner party.

Fish feast

- 4 oz (100 g) instant mashed potato pieces
- 1 medium onion, finely chopped
- 14.1 oz (400 g) can tuna in brine, drained
- 2 tablespoons chopped fresh parsley, or 2 teaspoons dried
- 2 oz (50 g) plain flour
- 6 eggs (size 3)
- 4 oz (100 g) rolled porridge oats
- vegetable oil for shallow frying

1 Make up mashed potato according to instructions.
2 Dry-fry onion in a large nonstick frying pan for 3 minutes until softened. Mash tuna and stir into mashed potato with onion and parsley. Season well.
3 With wetted hands, divide fish mixture into eight equal portions and shape into 3 inch (7.5 cm) fishcakes. Put on a baking sheet and freeze for 15 minutes until firm.
4 Season flour. Beat 2 eggs. Dip fishcakes into flour, then beaten egg and coat with rolled oats.
5 Heat oil for shallow frying in a heavy-based frying pan and cook fishcakes in two batches for 10 minutes each, turning once.
6 Remove fishcakes. Drain on kitchen paper and keep hot.
7 Fry remaining eggs in oil for 3 minutes or until set. Serve eggs and fishcakes with baked beans. Garnish with flat leaf parsley and serve with tomato relish.

TIME: *preparation 20 minutes; freezing 15 minutes; cooking 26 minutes*
NUTRIENTS PER SERVING: *Calories 580; Total fat 20 g; Fibre 4 g; Carbohydrate 50 g*

FOOD EDITOR'S TIP

These are perfect for making in batches and keeping in the freezer.

Salmon courgette flan

- 8 oz (225 g) frozen shortcrust pastry, thawed
- 14 oz (397 g) can pink salmon in oil
- 1 onion, thinly sliced
- 8 oz (225 g) courgettes, sliced
- 10.4 oz (295 g) can condensed celery soup
- 3 eggs (size 3)

1 Roll out pastry and use to line a 9 inch (23 cm) flan tin. Prick base with a fork and chill for 10 minutes. Bake blind at 375°F (190°C), Gas 5 for 10 minutes. Remove lining and cook for 10 minutes.
2 Meanwhile, drain salmon, reserving oil. Heat 1 tablespoon of the oil in a frying pan. Add onion, cook for 3 minutes until soft. Add courgettes, cover and cook for 4 minutes until tender. Drain oil and place onion and courgettes in pastry case.
3 Break salmon into large chunks. Remove all skin and bones and put fish into pastry case.
4 Whisk together soup and eggs, pour over filling. Cook at 375°F (190°C), Gas 5 for 45 minutes. Garnish with parsley sprigs, serve with oven chips, peas and grilled tomatoes.

TIME: *preparation 20 minutes; chilling 10 minutes; cooking 1 hour 5 minutes*
NUTRIENTS PER SERVING: *Calories 560; Total fat 35 g; Fibre 2 g; Carbohydrate 34 g*

FOOD EDITOR'S TIP

You can make this in advance, refrigerate and reheat for 1 minute on full power in the microwave.

FAST TO COOK

Coronation chicken

- 12 oz (325 g) basmati rice
- 1¼ lb (550 g) cooked chicken
- 2 tablespoons vegetable oil
- 1 onion, finely chopped
- 2 tablespoons mild curry paste
- 1 teaspoon ground coriander
- 1 teaspoon tomato purée
- 14½ oz (411 g) can apricots in natural juice, drained
- 10 fl oz (284 ml) mayonnaise
- 5 oz (125 g) Greek strained yogurt
- 1 tablespoon coriander leaves

1. Wash rice and put in saucepan with a little salt. Cover with cold water and bring to boil. Reduce heat, stir and cook for 20 minutes.
2. Remove chicken skin. Chop meat into large chunks.
3. Heat oil in pan, fry onion for 5 minutes. Reduce heat, stir in curry paste, coriander and tomato purée. Cook for 5 minutes.
4. Mash half the apricots with a fork and stir into pan with onions. Remove from heat and cool. Transfer paste to a large bowl and stir in mayonnaise and yogurt. Fold in chicken with coriander leaves.
5. Drain rice. Slice remaining apricots, stir into rice and serve.

TIME: *preparation 20 minutes; cooking 20 minutes*
NUTRIENTS PER SERVING: *Calories 1160; Total fat 72 g; Fibre 3g; Carbohydrate 82 g*

FOOD EDITOR'S TIP

Try adding celery and walnuts for extra crunch.

Hot chicken salad

- 10 oz (275 g) cold cooked chicken, diced
- 2 oz (50 g) American-style wafer-thin pastrami slices
- 4 spring onions, chopped
- 3 sticks celery, sliced
- 4 oz (100 g) frozen sweetcorn, thawed
- 5 fl oz (142 ml) mayonnaise
- 2 tablespoons lemon juice
- 3 oz (75 g) cheddar, grated
- pinch paprika
- 3 tablespoons olive oil
- 3½ oz (100 g) packet mixed salad leaves
- ½ iceberg lettuce, torn into bite-sized pieces

1 Put diced chicken, pastrami, spring onions, celery, sweetcorn, mayonnaise and 1 tablespoon lemon juice into a bowl. Mix together then stir in 2 oz (50 g) cheddar and seasoning.

2 Spoon mixture into a shallow ovenproof dish. Sprinkle with remaining cheese and paprika. Cook at 425°F (220°C), Gas 7 for 15 minutes until cheese has melted and browned and chicken is piping hot.

3 Meanwhile, whisk remaining lemon juice, oil and seasoning in a salad bowl. Add salad leaves and lettuce and toss. Serve with hot crusty rolls.

TIME: *preparation 15 minutes; cooking 15 minutes*
NUTRIENTS PER SERVING: *Calories 475; Total fat 38 g; Fibre 1 g; Carbohydrate 6 g*

FOOD EDITOR'S TIP

The pastrami adds a lovely spicy flavour but you could use wafer-thin ham slices if you prefer.

Sizzling chicken

- 4 x 6 oz (150 g) boneless chicken breasts
- 1 teaspoon cornflour
- ¼ teaspoon chilli seasoning
- 1 packet mixed peppers, deseeded and thickly sliced
- 2 medium onions, sliced
- 1 green chilli, deseeded and sliced
- 3 tablespoons sunflower oil

1 Flatten each chicken breast slightly by beating with a rolling pin. Cut each breast lengthways into four.

2 Put chicken in a single layer on a chopping board. Mix together cornflour and chilli seasoning and dust lightly over chicken.

3 Fry peppers, onions and chilli in 1 tablespoon oil over a high heat for 4-5 minutes, stirring frequently. Remove from pan but keep warm.

4 Add remaining oil to pan and fry chicken in two batches over high heat for 5 minutes each, turning frequently until golden brown.

5 Return vegetables to chicken in pan to reheat for 2 minutes. Serve with guacamole and tortilla chips.

TIME: *preparation 20 minutes; cooking 12 minutes*
NUTRIENTS PER SERVING: *Calories 310; Total fat 16 g; Fibre 2 g; Carbohydrate 10 g*

FOOD EDITOR'S TIP

Guacamole is a creamy avocado mixture which is delicious with this recipe. Look for it in jars with the Mexican products at the supermarket.

Herby chicken

- 6 oz (150 g) butter
- 1 garlic clove, crushed
- 2 tablespoons chopped fresh herbs
- 4 x 6 oz (150 g) boneless chicken breasts
- 2 oz (50 g) plain flour
- 1 egg (size 3), beaten
- 4 oz (100 g) fresh breadcrumbs

1 Mix together butter, garlic and herbs, and season well. Chill for 15 minutes.
2 Make a deep slit in each chicken breast. Put flour, egg and breadcrumbs in three separate shallow bowls.
3 Push chilled butter into slits in chicken. Secure slits with cocktail sticks. Dip chicken pieces in flour, then egg and breadcrumbs, coating completely.
4 Cook at 375°F (175°C), Gas 5 for 30 minutes, until golden. Remove sticks. Serve with sautéd potatoes, peas, corn and tomato.

TIME: *preparation 15 minutes; chilling 15 minutes; cooking 30 minutes*
NUTRIENTS PER SERVING: *Calories 430; Total fat 26 g; Fibre 0 g; Carbohydrate 13 g*

FOOD EDITOR'S TIP

Try lining your baking dish with foil to catch any melted butter.

French bread chicken pizza

- 1 tablespoon vegetable oil
- 1 onion, sliced
- ½ each red and green pepper, deseeded and sliced
- 1 tablespoon tomato purée
- 7 oz (198 g) can chopped tomatoes
- 12 oz (325 g) lean cooked chicken, diced
- ½ French stick
- 14 oz (400 g) can artichoke hearts, drained
- 4 oz (100 g) mozzarella
- 1 tablespoon poppy seeds

1 Heat oil in frying pan, gently fry onion and peppers for 7-8 minutes, until soft.
2 Stir in tomato purée, chopped tomatoes and chicken. Cook for 4 minutes. Remove from heat.
3 Cut French stick in half lengthways and then in half again. Spoon cooked tomato and chicken mixture on to each quarter. Cut artichoke hearts in half and arrange on top.
4 Slice mozzarella and arrange over chicken and artichoke mixture. Sprinkle with poppy seeds and cook under a preheated grill for 5 minutes until cheese has melted. Serve with green salad.

TIME: *preparation 20 minutes; cooking 17 minutes*
NUTRIENTS PER SERVING: *Calories 420; Total fat 15 g; Fibre 4 g; Carbohydrate 38 g*

FOOD EDITOR'S TIP

Freeze the leftovers next time you have roast chicken as they are ideal for making this pizza.

Ginger chicken stir-fry

- 2 inch (5 cm) piece fresh root ginger
- 1 tablespoon sesame oil
- 1 tablespoon olive oil
- 4 x 4 oz (100 g) fresh chicken breasts, skinned and cut into strips
- 1 red pepper, halved and deseeded
- 8 oz (225 g) broccoli, cut into small florets
- 1 bunch spring onions, chopped
- 1 oz (25 g) flaked almonds

1 Peel and finely shred ginger. Heat oils in a large frying pan or wok. Add ginger and chicken pieces, stir-fry over a high heat for 5 minutes.
2 Remove ginger and meat from pan. Add pepper, broccoli, spring onions and almonds to pan and stir-fry for 3 minutes.
3 Return chicken to pan and stir-fry over a high heat for 1 minute. Serve with a savoury rice.

TIME: *preparation 15 minutes; cooking 9 minutes*
NUTRIENTS PER SERVING: *Calories 250; Total fat 14 g; Fibre 3 g; Carbohydrate 4 g*

FOOD EDITOR'S TIP

If you can't find any fresh root ginger you can use unsweetened ginger purée instead.

Turkey and nut stir-fry

- 5 oz (125 g) easy-cook basmati rice
- 12 oz (325 g) cooked turkey
- 2 tablespoons sunflower oil
- 2 oz (50 g) walnut pieces
- 1 garlic clove, crushed
- ½ oz (15 g) fresh root ginger, finely chopped
- 1 small red pepper, deseeded and cut into strips
- 3 oz (75 g) baby corn, halved lengthways
- 4 spring onions, cut into 1 inch (2.5 cm) pieces
- 3 oz (75 g) brown cap mushrooms, sliced
- 1 courgette, cut into matchsticks
- 2 tablespoons chicken stock
- 2 tablespoons dry sherry
- 2 tablespoons light soy sauce

1 Rinse rice in cold water. Put in a large pan with salted boiling water. Return to boil. Cook uncovered for 15 minutes or until tender.
2 Meanwhile, cut cooked turkey into medium-sized strips.
3 Heat oil in a wok or large frying pan. Add walnuts and stir-fry for 1 minute. Remove and set aside.
4 Add garlic and ginger to pan. Stir-fry for 1 minute. Add pepper, corn and onions. Stir-fry for 2 minutes. Add mushrooms and courgette. Stir-fry for a further 2 minutes.
5 Return walnuts to pan with chicken stock, sherry and soy sauce. Stir in turkey and stir-fry for 2 minutes until heated through.
6 Drain rice and serve with the stir-fry.

TIME: *preparation 20 minutes; cooking 15 minutes*
NUTRIENTS PER SERVING: *Calories 540; Total fat 19 g; Fibre 2 g; Carbohydrate 60 g*

FOOD EDITOR'S TIP

Use brown basmati rice to make this an even more wholesome meal with plenty of extra fibre.

Celtic pan-fry

- 1½ lb (675 g) potatoes, diced
- 1 oz (25 g) butter
- 2 tablespoons sunflower oil
- 1 leek, thinly sliced
- 4 oz (100 g) cooked cabbage
- 2 oz (50 g) brussels sprouts, thinly sliced
- ¼ teaspoon grated nutmeg

1 Cook diced potatoes in a large saucepan of lightly salted water. Bring to boil, cook for around 15 minutes until tender.
2 Meanwhile, melt butter with 2 tablespoons oil in a large nonstick frying pan. Add leek, cabbage and sprouts. Stir-fry for 5 minutes until softened.
3 Add potatoes, nutmeg and plenty of seasoning. Fry, turning frequently for 10 minutes until mixture is browned.
4 Cut pan-fry into wedges and serve with grilled sausages, bacon and tomatoes.

TIME: *preparation 10 minutes; cooking 25 minutes*
NUTRIENTS PER SERVING: *Calories 250; Total fat 12 g; Fibre 4 g; Carbohydrate 31 g*

FOOD EDITOR'S TIP

This is a perfect dish for using up any leftover vegetables.

Peppered pan-fry

- 2 oz (50 g) butter
- 2 tablespoons chopped fresh parsley
- 4 tablespoons freshly crushed black peppercorns
- 4 x 5 oz (125 g) sirloin steaks
- 4 x 3 oz (75 g) lamb noisettes
- 4 tomatoes, halved
- 2 bulbs garlic, halved horizontally

1 Beat together butter and parsley. Season well. Put parsley butter on to a sheet of kitchen foil and roll up to form a thick sausage. Chill in fridge.
2 Meanwhile, put crushed peppercorns on a plate. Press steaks on to peppercorns to coat completely.
3 Dry-fry lamb noisettes, tomatoes and garlic bulbs in a nonstick frying pan for 10 minutes, turning once. Remove from pan and keep warm. Dry-fry steak for 5 minutes for rare, 7 minutes for medium, 10 minutes for well done, turning occasionally.
4 Unwrap butter, slice into four and put a circle of butter on to each lamb noisette. Serve peppered steak and lamb noisettes with sautéd potatoes, sweetcorn sprinkled with chopped fresh parsley, half a garlic bulb and a halved tomato. Garnish with a sprig of fresh rosemary.

TIME: *preparation 10 minutes; cooking 20 minutes*
NUTRIENTS PER SERVING: *Calories 650 g; Total fat 44 g; Fibre 1 g; Carbohydrate 2 g*

FOOD EDITOR'S TIP

Watch the lamb closely when dry-frying as it can burn quickly.

Pork paprikash

- 2 tablespoons olive oil
- 1 onion, thinly sliced
- 2 carrots, finely diced
- 1 lb (450 g) pork fillet, thinly sliced
- 4 oz (100 g) button mushrooms, quartered
- 1 garlic clove, crushed
- 1 teaspoon paprika
- 1 teaspoon caraway seeds
- 14 oz (397 g) can chopped tomatoes
- 5 fl oz (142 ml) chicken stock
- 2½ fl oz (71 ml) soured cream
- 1 teaspoon cornflour

1 Heat olive oil in a saucepan. Add onion and carrots and fry for 3 minutes until softened.

2 Add pork and mushrooms to pan. Fry until pork is evenly browned. Add crushed garlic and paprika, cook for 1 minute.

3 Add caraway seeds, tomatoes, chicken stock and seasoning. Bring to the boil, stirring. Cover and simmer for 10 minutes.

4 Remove pork from heat. Mix soured cream with cornflour. Stir into pork mixture and cook, stirring continuously, for 1 minute until thickened slightly.

5 Spoon into a warmed serving dish. Sprinkle with paprika and serve with creamy mashed potato and cabbage.

TIME: *preparation 25 minutes; cooking 18 minutes*
NUTRIENTS PER SERVING: *Calories 310; Total fat 18 g; Fibre 2 g; Carbohydrate 41 g*

FOOD EDITOR'S TIP

Trimmed and sliced pork spare rib chops can be used instead of pork fillet for a cheaper version.

Sausage spring salad

- 1½ lb (675 g) new potatoes, quartered
- 1 lb (450 g) pork sausages
- 6 oz (150 g) frozen broad beans
- 6 oz (150 g) asparagus sprue, trimmed and halved
- 4 oz (100 g) cherry tomatoes, halved
- 4 tablespoons olive oil
- 2 tablespoons white wine vinegar
- 1 tablespoon coarse grain mustard
- 1 teaspoon fennel seeds

1 Put potatoes in saucepan, cover with cold water, bring to boil and simmer for 20 minutes until tender.

2 Meanwhile, grill sausages for 10 minutes, turning until cooked evenly and cook beans in salted boiling water for 4 minutes. Add asparagus and cook for a further 4 minutes until vegetables are tender. Drain and put into salad bowl with tomatoes.

3 Whisk together thoroughly olive oil, white wine vinegar, mustard and fennel seeds. Pour dressing over vegetables.

4 Slice each sausage diagonally into three pieces. Add to the salad and toss together gently until well mixed. Serve salad warm with fresh crusty bread.

TIME: *preparation 25 minutes; cooking 20 minutes*
NUTRIENTS PER SERVING: *Calories 550; Total fat 35 g; Fibre 6 g; Carbohydrate 44 g*

FOOD EDITOR'S TIP

Use spiced sausages for a more peppery taste.

Crispy cauli-cheese

- 2 cauliflowers, cut into florets
- 1 pint (568 ml) skimmed milk
- 4 tablespoons cornflour
- 4 oz (100 g) mature cheddar, grated
- 4 oz (100 g) red leicester, grated
- 4 oz (100 g) smoked back bacon rashers
- 1 oz (25 g) fresh white breadcrumbs

1 Wash cauliflower florets, cook in a large pan of boiling water for 10 minutes.
2 Meanwhile, put all but 4 tablespoons milk into a pan and bring to boil, remove from heat. Mix reserved milk with cornflour to form a smooth paste. Gradually pour in hot milk. Season.
3 Return to pan, stir over a low heat for 5 minutes until thickened, add all but ½ oz (15 g) of each cheese. Remove from heat. Grill bacon for 5 minutes, turning once, until just crisp. Chop.
4 Drain cauliflower, divide between four 10 fl oz (284 ml) ovenproof dishes. Pour sauce over, then scatter with bacon, breadcrumbs and reserved cheeses. Grill for 5 minutes. Serve with a mixed salad and extra grated red leicester. Garnish with chopped fresh parsley.

TIME: *preparation 15 minutes; cooking 15 minutes*
NUTRIENTS PER SERVING: *Calories 550; Total fat 28 g; Fibre 9 g; Carbohydrate 34 g*

FOOD EDITOR'S TIP

To serve as a vegetable accompaniment omit the bacon and reduce the recipe by half.

Pork in cider sauce

- 2 oz (50 g) butter
- 2 dessert apples, peeled, cored and each sliced into 6 pieces
- 8 oz (225 g) button mushrooms, thinly sliced
- 10 fl oz (284 ml) dry cider
- 4 x 5 oz (125 g) pork steaks, trimmed
- 10 fl oz (284 ml) single cream

1 Melt butter in a frying pan, add apples and cook until golden. Remove with slotted spoon. Keep hot. Add mushrooms and cook until golden, remove and drain on kitchen paper.
2 Pour cider into pan, bring to boil and boil until reduced by half. Meanwhile, cook pork steaks under preheated grill for 6 minutes each side until tender and juices run clear when pierced with a skewer.
3 Add cream to reduced cider, return to boil. Simmer until thickened. Stir in reserved mushrooms and season well. Pour sauce over pork steaks. Serve pork and apples with sautéd potatoes, steamed broccoli and carrots.

TIME: *preparation 20 minutes; cooking 25 minutes*
NUTRIENTS PER SERVING: *Calories 450; Total fat 32 g; Fibre 1 g; Carbohydrate 11 g*

FOOD EDITOR'S TIP

If you think the apple flavour is too much for your family's taste, try substituting 5 fl oz (142 ml) stock for half the cider.

Crispy bacon salad

- 12 oz (325 g) new potatoes, scrubbed
- 4 oz (100 g) smoked streaky bacon, derinded
- 5 oz (125 g) carton natural yogurt
- 5 tablespoons mayonnaise
- 1 lb (450 g) cooked chicken pieces
- 2 avocados
- 4 oz (100 g) cherry tomatoes, halved
- 7 oz (200 g) bag mixed salad leaves
- ½ cucumber, sliced

1 Put potatoes in a pan, cover with cold water and bring to boil. Cover and simmer for 15 minutes. Drain and cool. Cut into bite-sized pieces. Grill bacon until crispy. Cool, roughly chop.

2 In a bowl, mix together yogurt and mayonnaise with seasoning. Stir in chicken and potatoes. Halve, stone, peel and chop avocados, add to chicken mixture.

3 Arrange cherry tomatoes, salad leaves and sliced cucumber on serving plates. Spoon chicken mixture on top. Sprinkle each plate with crispy bacon before serving.

TIME: *preparation 15 minutes; cooking 15 minutes*
NUTRIENTS PER SERVING: *Calories 610; Total fat 45 g; Fibre 1 g; Carbohydrate 22 g*

FOOD EDITOR'S TIP

Try serving this really hearty main meal salad just with crusty bread.

Deli platter

- 1 ciabatta loaf
- 4 oz (100 g) mature cheddar, grated
- 1 garlic clove, crushed
- pinch of dried mixed herbs
- 2 tablespoons milk
- 1 tablespoon olive oil
- 3 oz (80 g) packet sliced mortadella
- 2½ oz (70 g) packet sliced Prosciutto di Speck
- 2½ oz (70 g) packet sliced Milano salami
- 4 eggs (size 3), hard-boiled, shelled and quartered
- 2 tablespoons virgin olive oil
- 1 teaspoon black peppercorns, crushed

1 Make deep slits about 1 inch (2.5 cm) apart in ciabatta loaf. Mix together cheddar, garlic, herbs, milk and olive oil to form a smooth paste.

2 Spread cheese paste into each slit of ciabatta. Bake at 400°F (200°C), Gas 6 for 10 minutes.

3 Meanwhile, arrange meats and eggs on four plates. Drizzle over virgin olive oil, sprinkle with crushed peppercorns. Serve the hot, cheesy ciabatta with sliced cucumber, spring onions and salad leaves.

TIME: *preparation 10 minutes; cooking 10 minutes*
NUTRIENTS PER SERVING: *Calories 680; Total fat 43 g; Fibre 6 g; Carbohydrate 44 g*

FOOD EDITOR'S TIP

If you can't buy ciabatta bread, use a French stick instead.

Cheesy leek bake

- 8 medium leeks, trimmed
- 2 pints (1.1 litres) boiling water
- 8 slices honey roast ham
- 2 oz (50 g) butter
- 2 oz (50 g) plain flour
- 1 pint (568 ml) semi-skimmed milk
- 2 oz (50 g) cheddar, grated
- pinch of ground nutmeg
- 1 oz (25 g) flaked almonds

1 Wash leeks thoroughly under running water to remove any soil. Tie leeks with string to retain their shape. Cook in salted boiling water for 8 minutes until soft. Drain. Carefully untie string and discard. Wrap a slice of ham around each leek and put in base of a 3 pint (1.7 litre) shallow flameproof dish. Preheat grill to high.

2 Melt butter in a saucepan. Remove pan from heat and stir in flour. Return to a low heat and stir continuously for 1 minute or until a thick paste is formed and leaves the sides of the saucepan easily. Remove from heat, then gradually stir in the milk.

3 Stir over a medium heat for 3-4 minutes or until sauce thickens and boils. Stir in half the cheddar, nutmeg and seasoning. Stir over low heat for 1 minute until melted.

4 Pour sauce over leeks. Sprinkle over remaining cheddar and flaked almonds. Cook under hot grill for 3 minutes or until golden and bubbling.

5 Serve Cheesy Leek Bake with a mixed green salad.

TIME: *preparation 20 minutes; cooking 11 minutes*
NUTRIENTS PER SERVING: *Calories 420; Total fat 25 g; Fibre 4 g; Carbohydrate 22 g*

FOOD EDITOR'S TIP

Sprinkle fried breadcrumbs over the cheese sauce for extra crunch.

Parsley ham pasta

- 2 tablespoons olive oil
- 12 oz (325 g) dried tagliatelle verde
- 12 oz (325 g) button mushrooms, halved
- 1 small onion, sliced
- 2 garlic cloves, crushed
- 8 slices honey roast ham, cut into thick strips
- 5 fl oz (142 ml) single cream
- 5 oz (125 g) carton natural yogurt
- 4 tablespoons chopped fresh parsley
- 2 oz (50 g) cheddar, finely grated

1 Bring a large pan of salted water to the boil. Add 1 tablespoon olive oil and pasta. Cook for 8 minutes until tender or as directed on packet. Drain.

2 Meanwhile, fry mushrooms, onion and garlic in remaining oil for 5 minutes until soft.

3 Add honey roast ham, single cream, yogurt and seasoning to mushroom mixture. Stir over a low heat for 3 minutes, but do not allow to boil.

4 Add tagliatelle to ham mixture and toss gently with chopped fresh parsley and finely grated cheddar. Serve with extra grated cheese.

TIME: *preparation 20 minutes; cooking 8 minutes*
NUTRIENTS PER SERVING: *Calories 570; Total fat 23 g; Fibre 6 g; Carbohydrate 66 g*

FOOD EDITOR'S TIP

If you are watching calories, use low-fat fromage frais in place of the single cream.

Peppered noisettes

- 8 x 4 oz (100 g) lamb cutlets
- 1 tablespoon orange juice
- 1 tablespoon clear honey
- 4 oz (100 g) butter
- 1 teaspoon black peppercorns, crushed

1 Trim fat from cutlets and reserve. Using a very sharp small knife, remove bone from base of each. Wrap single flap of fat around the eye of the meat to form a noisette. Secure in place with cocktail sticks.

2 Mix together the orange juice and honey and brush a little over each noisette.

3 Cook noisettes under a medium grill for 8-10 minutes, turning frequently and brushing with remaining orange and honey glaze.

4 Meanwhile, beat together butter and peppercorns. Using a piece of dampened greaseproof paper, form butter into a roll then cut into eight slices.

5 Serve lamb noisettes topped with peppered butter with pommes noisettes, minted peas and cherry tomatoes. Garnish with mint.

TIME: *preparation 15 minutes; cooking 10 minutes*
NUTRIENTS PER SERVING: *Calories 340; Total fat 28 g; Fibre 0 g; Carbohydrate 3 g*

FOOD EDITOR'S TIP

You can also make the herb butter using chopped fresh mint or parsley instead of peppercorns.

Stilton grilled lamb

- 4 frozen lamb chump chops, thawed
- 1½ oz (40 g) walnut pieces
- 4 oz (100 g) stilton, derinded and diced

1 Season chops and cook under a hot grill for about 12 minutes, turning once.

2 Lay a sheet of foil over grill rack and put chops on top. Sprinkle with walnuts and stilton. Cook for 3 minutes until cheese has just melted.

3 Serve lamb with scalloped potatoes, peas and grilled tomatoes, garnished with parsley.

TIME: *preparation 15 minutes; cooking 15 minutes*
NUTRIENTS PER SERVING: *Calories 350; Total fat 35 g; Fibre Trace; Carbohydrate Trace*

FOOD EDITOR'S TIP

Look for a good quality stilton. It should be moist and crumble easily.

Seaside kebabs

- 8 oz (225 g) hoki fillet, skinned
- 12 oz (325 g) salmon fillet, skinned
- 1 green pepper, deseeded and cut into squares
- 16 button mushrooms
- 1 lemon, grated rind and juice
- 2 tablespoons olive oil
- ¼ teaspoon black peppercorns, crushed

1. Wash fish and pat dry on kitchen paper. Remove any bones from each fillet and cut flesh into bite-sized pieces.
2. Thread hoki and salmon alternately on to eight wooden kebab skewers with green pepper squares and button mushrooms. Mix together half of grated lemon rind with juice, oil and peppercorns. Brush over kebabs.
3. Cook kebabs under a preheated grill for 10-12 minutes, turning frequently and brushing with oil mixture. Put on to serving plates. Serve with rice and peas, garnished with remaining lemon rind and fresh dill.

TIME: *preparation 15 minutes; cooking 12 minutes*
NUTRIENTS PER SERVING: *Calories 260; Total fat 17 g; Fibre 1 g; Carbohydrate 1 g*

FOOD EDITOR'S TIP

If hoki is difficult to find, use another firm, white fish such as cod.

Minted lamb kebabs

- 1 aubergine, thickly sliced and halved
- 1 oz (25 g) salt
- 1½ lb (675 g) lean minced lamb
- 1 tablespoon mild chilli seasoning
- 1 garlic clove, crushed
- 1 small onion, finely chopped
- 1 tablespoon chopped fresh mixed herbs
- 1 orange, thickly sliced and halved
- 8 oz (225 g) natural low-fat yogurt
- 1 teaspoon mint sauce

1. Sprinkle aubergine with salt, leave for 15 minutes. Meanwhile, mix together mince, chilli seasoning, garlic, onion and herbs. Season.
2. Using your hands, shape meat into twelve balls. Rinse and pat dry aubergine. Thread meat alternately on to four skewers with halved aubergine and orange slices. Grill for 12 minutes, turning once.
3. Meanwhile, mix together low-fat yogurt and mint sauce. Spoon into a bowl. Chill until ready to serve.
4. Remove skewers and place kebabs on a bed of wild and long grain rice, garnished with fresh coriander. Serve with a mixed salad.

TIME: *preparation 20 minutes; cooking 12 minutes*
NUTRIENTS PER SERVING: *Calories 580; Total fat 18 g; Fibre 5 g; Carbohydrate 66 g*

FOOD EDITOR'S TIP

You should find these fine, even for kids, as chilli seasoning isn't nearly as hot as chilli powder.

Seafood bake

- 2 lb (900 g) potatoes, sliced
- 1 oz (25 g) butter
- 2 tablespoons vegetable oil
- 2 medium onions, finely chopped
- ½ teaspoon paprika
- 1 pint (568 ml) carton tomato soup
- 1 lb (450 g) cod fillet, skinned and boned
- 7 oz (198 g) can sweetcorn, drained
- 4 oz (100 g) frozen peeled prawns, thawed
- 1 oz (25 g) mature cheddar, grated

1 Boil potatoes in lightly salted water for 15 minutes. Drain and mash with butter, season well.
2 Meanwhile, heat oil and fry onions with paprika for 3 minutes until soft. Pour in soup, simmer for 5 minutes. Roughly chop cod and add to soup with sweetcorn, simmer for 5 minutes. Stir in prawns, simmer for 5 minutes, season well.
3 Divide fish mixture between four 10 fl oz (284 ml) ovenproof dishes. Spoon potato around fish mixture. Sprinkle potato with cheddar and grill for 5 minutes. Garnish with chopped parsley and lime wedges.

TIME: *preparation 20 minutes; cooking 23 minutes*
NUTRIENTS PER SERVING: *Calories 440; Total fat 17 g; Fibre 4 g; Carbohydrate 46 g*

FOOD EDITOR'S TIP

Look out for tail end pieces of cod – these are inexpensive and have few bones.

Florentine cod

- 8 oz (225 g) fresh spinach
- 4 x 3½ oz (90 g) frozen cod portions, thawed
- 1 tablespoon white wine vinegar
- 2 tablespoons lemon juice
- 6 oz (150 g) butter
- 3 egg yolks (size 3)
- 1 teaspoon caster sugar

1 Remove stalks from spinach leaves. Wash, steam for 1 minute and drain on kitchen paper.
2 Season cod, wrap each portion in spinach leaves. Steam for 8 minutes until fish is tender.
3 Meanwhile, to make hollandaise sauce: put vinegar and lemon juice into a small pan and heat to just below boiling point. In a separate pan, melt butter over a low heat.
4 Put egg yolks and sugar into a food processor and blend for 30 seconds. While machine is still running, add hot vinegar mixture then the melted butter in a slow stream.
5 Serve fish parcels with steamed new potatoes, baby carrots, French beans and hollandaise sauce garnished with lemon and dill.

TIME: *preparation 20 minutes; cooking 9 minutes*
NUTRIENTS PER SERVING: *Calories 400; Total fat 36 g; Fibre 1 g; Carbohydrate 2 g*

FOOD EDITOR'S TIP

Always dry spinach leaves really well as they hold a lot of water.

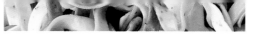

Salmon puffs

- 8 oz (225 g) sheet frozen puff pastry, thawed
- 1 egg (size 3), beaten
- 8 oz (225 g) tail end salmon fillet
- 4 tablespoons dry white wine
- 6 oz (150 g) button mushrooms, wiped
- ½ oz (15 g) butter
- ½ tablespoon cornflour
- 10 fl oz (284 ml) milk
- 2 tablespoons chopped fresh dill

1 Roll out puff pastry to an 8 x 5 inch (20.5 x 12.5 cm) rectangle. Cut into quarters to form four 4 x 2½ inch (10 x 6.5 cm) rectangles.
2 Brush with beaten egg. Score surface of each lightly with a sharp knife. Cook at 425°F (220°C), Gas 7 for 10 minutes until puffy and golden.
3 Meanwhile, trim and wash fish. Cut into bite-sized cubes. Put on to a small baking sheet and sprinkle over half the wine. Cook in oven with pastry for 8-10 minutes or until tender.
4 Meanwhile, cook mushrooms in butter for 5 minutes until tender. Mix together remaining wine and cornflour to form a smooth paste.
5 Add milk to mushrooms and bring to the boil. Stir in the wine mixture and stir over low heat until sauce has thickened. Stir in cooked salmon, seasoning and dill.
6 Spoon salmon mixture on to serving plates and top with pastry lid. Serve with duchesse potatoes, steamed runner beans and sweetcorn with mixed peppers.

TIME: *preparation 20 minutes; cooking 10 minutes*
NUTRIENTS PER SERVING: *Calories 400; Total fat 25 g; Fibre 0 g; Carbohydrate 26 g*

FOOD EDITOR'S TIP

If you're not wine drinkers, you can buy just a single 9 fl oz (250 ml) can for this recipe.

Seafood spaghetti

- 1 tablespoon olive oil
- 1 each small red and green pepper, deseeded and diced
- 1 garlic clove, crushed
- 13 oz (376 g) can cream and white wine sauce
- 12 oz (325 g) spaghetti
- 14 oz (400 g) packet frozen seafood cocktail, thawed

1 Heat oil in a large pan and fry peppers and garlic over a low heat for 5 minutes. Stir in cream and white wine sauce and simmer for 5 minutes.
2 Meanwhile, bring a large pan of lightly salted water to the boil and add spaghetti. Cook for 8 minutes or according to packet instructions.
3 Drain seafood cocktail and rinse under cold running water. Add to sauce and bring to the boil, stirring continuously.
4 Reduce heat and cook for 5 minutes, stirring occasionally, until seafood is heated through. Drain spaghetti and spoon seafood on top. Serve with grated fresh parmesan and garnish with fresh chervil.

TIME: *preparation 15 minutes; cooking 23 minutes*
NUTRIENTS PER SERVING: *Calories 490; Total fat 12 g; Fibre 3 g; Carbohydrate 70 g*

FOOD EDITOR'S TIP

This is a really adaptable recipe. Served in smaller portions, it also makes an ideal starter.

Penne rigate

- 1 tablespoon olive oil
- 1 onion, chopped
- 1 garlic clove, crushed
- 14 oz (397 g) can chopped tomatoes
- 2 tablespoons tomato purée
- 12 oz (325 g) penne rigate pasta
- 14.1 oz (400 g) can tuna chunks in brine, drained
- 3 oz (75 g) mozzarella, cubed
- 2 oz (50 g) stuffed green olives
- 2 oz (50 g) pitted black olives

1 Heat olive oil in frying pan, fry chopped onion for 3 minutes until soft. Add garlic, reduce heat and fry for a further 2 minutes or until softened. Stir in tomatoes and tomato purée, season well and simmer, uncovered, for 10 minutes or until sauce has thickened.
2 Meanwhile, bring a large pan of lightly salted water to the boil. Cook pasta for 10 minutes or until tender.
3 Add tuna chunks to tomato sauce with mozzarella, green olives and black olives. Simmer for 5 minutes.
4 Drain pasta and season with freshly ground black pepper, then divide between four serving plates. Spoon tuna and tomato sauce over top of pasta. Garnish with grated fresh parmesan and fresh basil leaves. Serve with mixed salad leaves.

TIME: *preparation 15 minutes; cooking 20 minutes*
NUTRIENTS PER SERVING: *Calories 670; Total fat 30 g; Fibre 5 g; Carbohydrate 68 g*

FOOD EDITOR'S TIP

The given weight of pasta is plenty for four people - don't be tempted to add any more as it swells up considerably when cooked.

Avocado with prawn salad

- 2 baby gem lettuces
- 4 oz (100 g) packet lambs lettuce
- 2 ripe avocados, stoned and peeled
- 4 rashers back bacon, cooked and shredded
- 4 oz (100 g) canned red kidney beans, rinsed and drained
- 4 oz (100 g) frozen peeled prawns, thawed
- 2 oz (50 g) mozzarella, cubed
- 1½ oz (40 g) packet garlic bread cocktail snacks
- 6 oz (150 g) cherry tomatoes, halved
- 2 oz (50 g) salted cashew nuts
- 1 teaspoon wholegrain mustard
- 1 garlic clove, crushed
- 2 tablespoons white wine vinegar
- 2 fl oz (57 ml) olive oil
- 1 tablespoon fresh parsley

1 Divide gem and lambs lettuce between four salad bowls.
2 Slice each avocado in half lengthways and fan out the pieces. Lay avocado in centre of bowls with the shredded bacon. Scatter kidney beans, prawns, mozzarella, garlic bread cocktail snacks, tomato halves and cashew nuts over the lettuce.
3 In a bowl, beat together mustard, crushed garlic, vinegar, oil and chopped parsley to make a thick dressing. Either pour over salad and toss well or pour into a jug and serve separately.

TIME: *preparation 20 minutes*
NUTRIENTS PER SERVING: *Calories 570; Total fat 46 g; Fibre 6 g; Carbohydrate 17 g*

FOOD EDITOR'S TIP

If garlic bread snacks are unavailable, make your own croûtons.

Prawn deckers

- 8 oz (225 g) frozen peeled prawns, thawed
- 2 teaspoons tomato ketchup
- 6 tablespoons mayonnaise
- 1 teaspoon Worcestershire sauce
- 6 slices Granary bread, toasted
- 6 slices high-grain bread, toasted
- 2 inch (5 cm) piece cucumber, thinly sliced
- 6 oz (150 g) cottage cheese with mixed peppers
- 1 oz (25 g) watercress, stems removed
- 2 tomatoes, sliced

1 Mix together prawns, ketchup, mayonnaise and Worcestershire sauce. Season. Remove crusts from bread. Take two slices of each bread, spoon over prawn mixture and cucumber.
2 Spread cottage cheese over two slices of each bread and place these cheese side up on top of prawns. Top with watercress and tomatoes. Season, top with remaining toast.
3 Cut decks into four. Fix together with cocktail sticks and chill. Serve with crisps and mixed carrot coleslaw topped with almonds. Remove cocktail sticks before eating.

TIME: *preparation 20 minutes*
NUTRIENTS PER SERVING: *Calories 790; Total fat 34 g; Fibre 16 g; Carbohydrate 92 g*

FOOD EDITOR'S TIP

You can use ready-made thousand island dressing for the prawns to save time.

Sesame fish stir-fry

- 1 lb (450 g) cod fillets, skinned
- 1 oz (25 g) plain flour
- 1 egg (size 3), beaten
- 3 oz (75 g) sesame seeds
- 2 tablespoons sesame oil
- ¼ red cabbage, finely shredded
- 6 oz (150 g) carrots, cut into matchsticks
- 8 oz (225 g) courgettes, sliced diagonally
- 2 leeks, sliced thinly
- 12 oz (325 g) spinach, roughly torn
- 8 oz (225 g) beansprouts

1 Cut cod fillets into bite-sized pieces. Season flour and put into a polybag with fish. Shake gently to coat each piece.
2 Cover cod pieces with beaten egg and coat well with sesame seeds. Spread out on a greased baking sheet and cook at 400°F (200°C), Gas 6 for 10-12 minutes until they are cooked through and pale golden brown in colour.
3 Meanwhile, heat sesame oil in a wok or large frying pan. Stir-fry shredded red cabbage, carrot matchsticks, sliced courgettes and leeks for 5 minutes until soft.
4 Add spinach leaves and beansprouts and stir-fry for 2 minutes. Stir in fish and spoon on to plates.

TIME: *preparation 20 minutes; cooking 12 minutes*
NUTRIENTS PER SERVING: *Calories 400; Total fat 21 g; Fibre 6 g; Carbohydrate 23 g*

FOOD EDITOR'S TIP

As an alternative, use a white or savoy cabbage if red is unavailable.

Fish parcels

- 4 x 5 oz (125 g) haddock tail fillets
- 12 stoned black olives
- 2 tomatoes, sliced
- 1 lime, grated rind and juice

1. Wash fish and pat dry. Cut four sheets of foil, large enough to wrap around each fillet to form a parcel. Put fish on foil.
2. Arrange tomato slices, 3 olives and grated lime rind over each fillet. Sprinkle over lime juice and season well.
3. Fold foil around fish, pinching edges together to seal. Put into base of a steamer set over a pan of water, bring to boil and steam for 6 minutes.
4. Put fish parcels on serving plates and serve with steamed courgettes, baby corn cobs and boiled potatoes. Put a knob of butter on to potatoes before serving.

TIME: *preparation 25 minutes; cooking 6 minutes*
NUTRIENTS PER SERVING: *Calories 100; Total fat 2 g; Fibre Trace; Carbohydrate 1 g*

FOOD EDITOR'S TIP

Use thawed frozen haddock fillets if fresh are difficult to find.

Supper kedgeree

- 12 oz (325 g) long grain rice
- 1 lb (450 g) smoked haddock fillet
- 10 fl oz (284 ml) milk
- ½ teaspoon ground nutmeg
- 4 eggs (size 3)
- 1 tablespoon oil
- 1 leek, washed and finely sliced
- 2 tablespoons chopped fresh dill, or 1 tablespoon dried

1. Wash rice. Cook in boiling salted water for 20 minutes.
2. Meanwhile, put haddock in large deep-sided frying pan and pour milk over. Sprinkle with nutmeg. Bring to boil, reduce heat and simmer for 15 minutes.
3. Boil eggs for 3½ minutes. Drain, run under cold water, shell and set aside. Heat oil in frying pan and fry chopped leek for 2 minutes.
4. Drain rice and stir into leeks. Drain haddock. Remove skin and bones then flake flesh using two forks. Stir fish into rice.
5. Quarter eggs and add to fish mixture. Add fresh or dried dill. Spoon on to four warm plates and serve garnished with sprigs of fresh dill, lemon wedges and melba toast triangles.

To make melba toast: toast four slices white bread. Cut off crusts. Using a sharp knife, cut through middle, splitting each into two, ending up with eight thin slices toasted on one side. Cut into triangles. Toast raw side until edges curl.

TIME: *preparation 20 minutes; cooking 20 minutes*
NUTRIENTS PER SERVING: *Calories 570; Total fat 14 g; Fibre 1 g; Carbohydrate 69 g*

FOOD EDITOR'S TIP

If you prefer a more moist kedgeree add a little cream to the rice.

Lemon crumbed fish and chips

- 5 oz (125 g) white breadcrumbs
- 1 lemon, grated rind only
- 1 tablespoon chopped fresh parsley
- 4 x 6 oz (150 g) plaice fillets
- 2 eggs (size 3), beaten
- 3 oz (75 g) plain flour
- 2 lb (900 g) potatoes, peeled
- oil for deep frying

1 Mix together breadcrumbs, grated lemon rind and parsley. Season and reserve.
2 Wash plaice fillets and dry on kitchen paper. Pour beaten eggs into a shallow dish, large enough to dip fillets into.
3 Put flour and seasoned breadcrumb mixture on two separate plates. Dip plaice fillets in flour then in beaten egg and coat with breadcrumb mixture.
4 Cut potatoes into chips. Heat oil in a 4 pint (2.3 litre) heavy-based saucepan or deep-fat fryer to 375°F (190°C), or until a cube of bread rises and sizzles within 30 seconds. Fry chips for 10 minutes. Remove chip basket and let oil reheat. Cook chips for a further 2 minutes until golden.
5 Meanwhile, grill plaice for 10 minutes, turning. Serve with tomatoes, parsley and lemon wedges.

TIME: *preparation 15 minutes; cooking 12 minutes*
NUTRIENTS PER SERVING: *Calories 600; Total fat 19 g; Fibre 2 g; Carbohydrate 73 g*

FOOD EDITOR'S TIP

It is useful to make double the amount of breadcrumbs and freeze some for another day.

Pissaladière

- 2½ tablespoons olive oil
- 1 onion, chopped
- 1 garlic clove, crushed
- 14 oz (397 g) can chopped tomatoes
- 2 tablespoons tomato purée
- 10½ oz (290 g) packet pizza base mix
- 1 yellow pepper, deseeded and chopped
- 2 x 2 oz (50 g) cans anchovy fillets, drained
- 2 oz (50 g) pitted black olives

1 Heat ½ tablespoon olive oil in frying pan, fry chopped onion for 3 minutes until soft. Add garlic and fry for a further 2 minutes. Stir in tomatoes and tomato purée, season well and simmer, uncovered, for 10 minutes or until sauce has thickened.
2 Put pizza base mix in a large bowl and make up as packet instructions. Knead for 5 minutes or until dough is smooth and elastic. Divide dough into four pieces and roll each out on a lightly floured surface to 6 inch (15 cm) rounds. Pinch up edges to form a rim. Brush dough with remaining olive oil.
3 Spread tomato sauce over pizza rounds to come within ½ inch (1.3 cm) of rim of dough. Top with chopped yellow pepper, anchovy fillets and black olives. Cook at 425°F (220°C), Gas 7 for 20 minutes. Garnish each Pissaladière with a sprig of fresh oregano and serve with a tomato salad.

TIME: *preparation 15 minutes; cooking 35 minutes*
NUTRIENTS PER SERVING: *Calories 460; Total fat 18 g; Fibre 2 g; Carbohydrate 58 g*

FOOD EDITOR'S TIP

Make sure you roll out the dough evenly to form the circles otherwise it will shrink during cooking.

FAST TO COOK

Mackerel salad

- 1 lb (450 g) small new potatoes, scrubbed
- 8 oz (225 g) French beans
- 2 x 8 oz (225 g) packets peppered smoked mackerel fillets
- ½ bunch spring onions, trimmed and finely sliced
- 2 x 7 oz (200 g) packets mixed salad leaves
- 4 tablespoons olive oil
- 1 tablespoon white wine vinegar
- 1 garlic clove, crushed

1 Put potatoes in a pan of salted water and bring to boil. Cook for 15 minutes or until tender. Steam French beans above potatoes for last 5 minutes of cooking time. Drain and cool. Break mackerel fillets into bite-sized pieces.

2 Arrange potatoes, French beans, mackerel pieces and spring onions in a shallow salad dish with salad leaves. Whisk together olive oil, vinegar and garlic. Season well and pour over salad just before serving.

TIME: *preparation 20 minutes; cooking 15 minutes*
NUTRIENTS PER SERVING: *Calories 470; Total fat 32 g; Fibre 6 g; Carbohydrate 22 g*

FOOD EDITOR'S TIP

Take care when seasoning the salad dressing as smoked mackerel has a lot of flavour and is very salty.

Plaice with wild rice

- 3 oz (75 g) mayonnaise
- few sprigs fresh dill, chopped
- 1 tablespoon capers, finely chopped
- 2 teaspoons lemon juice
- 2 pints (1.1 litres) vegetable stock
- 8 oz (225 g) easy-cook long grain and wild rice
- 4 x 5 oz (125 g) plaice fillets
- 2 oz (50 g) plain flour, seasoned
- 1 egg (size 3), beaten
- 4 oz (100 g) rolled porridge oats
- 6 tablespoons vegetable oil
- 2 oz (50 g) frozen sweetcorn, thawed

1 To make caper sauce: mix together mayonnaise, dill, capers and lemon juice. Chill.
2 Bring stock to boil, add rice and cook for 12 minutes or according to packet instructions.
3 Dip fish in flour, coat in egg and then oats.
4 Heat oil for shallow frying in a heavy-based frying pan and cook fish for 3 minutes each side. Drain on kitchen paper, keep hot.
5 Stir sweetcorn into rice, cover, leave for 2 minutes. Drain. Garnish fish with lemon slices and dill. Serve with caper sauce, rice and salad.

TIME: *preparation 15 minutes; cooking 26 minutes*
NUTRIENTS PER SERVING: *Calories 800; Total fat 42 g; Fibre 10 g; Carbohydrate 77 g*

FOOD EDITOR'S TIP

Make sure the oil is really hot before you begin to fry the fish.

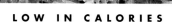

LOW IN CALORIES

Hawaiian burgers

- 8 oz (225 g) can pineapple rings in natural juice
- 3 tablespoons clear honey
- 2 tablespoons light soy sauce
- 1 teaspoon ground ginger
- 2 garlic cloves, crushed
- 4 x 4 oz (100 g) chicken breasts, skinned
- 4 wholemeal baps, split
- 2 tomatoes, sliced
- 4 lettuce leaves
- 1 small red chilli, deseeded and sliced
- 1 gherkin, finely sliced

1 Drain pineapple. Mix 2 tablespoons of juice with honey, soy sauce, ginger and garlic. Score chicken with a knife. Brush with glaze. Grill for 10 minutes, turn, glaze again. Cook for 10 minutes.

2 Put pineapple rings on top. Brush over any remaining glaze and grill for 5 minutes.

3 Meanwhile, toast baps. Divide 1 tomato, lettuce, chilli and gherkin between each. Put chicken and pineapple, remaining tomato and bap lids on top. Serve with chips, peas and spring onions. Garnish with fresh parsley and tomato wedges.

TIME: *preparation 15 minutes; cooking 25 minutes*
NUTRIENTS PER SERVING: *Calories 300; Total fat 5 g; Fibre 3 g; Carbohydrate 38 g*

Crispy chicken pie

- 6 oz (150 g) frozen chopped spinach
- 1 onion, finely sliced
- 2 garlic cloves, crushed
- 6 sheets filo pastry
- 8 oz (225 g) cooked chicken, roughly chopped
- 3 tomatoes, sliced
- 4 oz (100 g) low-fat cream cheese
- 1 egg (size 3), beaten
- 1 teaspoon cornflour

1 Cook spinach over a medium heat, stirring occasionally, for 5 minutes or until all liquid has evaporated. In a small nonstick saucepan, dry-fry onion and garlic for 5 minutes until softened. Stir in spinach. Season well.
2 Line an 8 inch (20 cm) flan tin with five sheets of filo pastry, ensuring pastry edges overlap across base and over sides of tin. Put a baking sheet in oven preheated to 350°F (180°C), Gas 4 to heat through.
3 Layer chicken, spinach mixture and tomato slices in pastry case. Season. Beat together cream cheese, beaten egg and cornflour, and spoon over filling. Fold pastry back over filling to cover surface completely. Cut remaining pastry sheet into long strips, scrunch together and arrange over pie.
4 Put flan tin on hot baking sheet and cook pie for 45 minutes until top is golden. Remove pie from oven and ease out of flan tin immediately. Garnish with flat leaf parsley.

TIME: *preparation 25 minutes; cooking 55 minutes*
NUTRIENTS PER SERVING: *Calories 240; Total fat 6 g; Fibre 4 g; Carbohydrate 23 g*

FOOD EDITOR'S TIP

Filo pastry dries out quickly so keep it well covered with a damp tea towel while making up the pie filling.

Chicken pan-soufflé

- 2 x 4 oz (100 g) boneless, skinless chicken breasts
- 1 leek, finely sliced
- 6 eggs (size 3), separated
- ¼ teaspoon cayenne pepper
- 2 tablespoons chopped fresh parsley

1 Slice chicken into bite-sized pieces. Dry-fry in an 8 inch (20.5 cm) nonstick frying pan for 8 minutes or until golden.
2 Add leek slices and cook for 3 minutes until softened. Remove chicken and leeks from pan and put into a bowl with egg yolks. Season with cayenne and a pinch of salt.
3 Whisk egg whites in a clean bowl until soft peaks form. Fold into chicken mixture with chopped parsley.
4 Spoon a quarter of chicken mixture into frying pan. Cook over a low heat for 4 minutes or until base is set. Grill for 2 minutes until top is soft and golden. Keep hot.
5 Repeat step 4 to make four soufflés in total. Serve with steamed broccoli and grilled tomatoes, garnished with flat leaf parsley.

TIME: *preparation 20 minutes; cooking 36 minutes*
NUTRIENTS PER SERVING: *Calories 210; Total fat 11 g; Fibre 1 g; Carbohydrate 1 g*

FOOD EDITOR'S TIP

Keep each cooked soufflé hot in the oven whilst preparing the rest.

Turkey paprika

- 1 tablespoon sunflower oil
- 4 x 4 oz (100 g) turkey escalopes
- 1 large onion, sliced
- 1 garlic clove, crushed
- 14 oz (397 g) can tomatoes
- 1½ tablespoons tomato purée
- ½ tablespoon paprika
- 1 red pepper, thinly sliced
- 4 fl oz (114 ml) chicken stock
- ½ savoy cabbage
- 1 small bunch watercress
- 1 teaspoon sesame seeds
- 1 teaspoon poppy seeds

1 Heat oil in frying pan. Fry escalopes for 1½ minutes each side until lightly browned. Set aside.
2 Fry onions and garlic for 5 minutes. Add tomatoes, purée and paprika. Cook for 20 minutes. Add turkey, red pepper and stock to pan. Cover and simmer for 20 minutes.
3 Meanwhile, shred cabbage leaves and steam for 6 minutes. Drain, stir in remaining ingredients. Serve with new potatoes. Garnish with mint.

TIME: *preparation 30 minutes; cooking 48 minutes*
NUTRIENTS PER SERVING: *Calories 280; Total fat 6 g; Fibre 6 g; Carbohydrate 29 g*

FOOD EDITOR'S TIP

Turkey breasts can be used in place of escalopes.

Chicken satay sticks

- 4 x 4 oz (100 g) boneless, skinless chicken breasts
- 1 garlic clove, crushed
- 1 lime, grated rind and juice
- 4 tablespoons Malaysian satay sauce

1 Soak sixteen 6 inch (15 cm) bamboo skewers in hot water. Beat chicken breasts one at a time in a polybag with a rolling pin until flattened slightly. Cut each into four strips.
2 Mix together garlic, lime rind and juice and satay sauce in a shallow dish. Add chicken, cover and leave to marinate for 1 hour.
3 Thread chicken on to skewers, reserving marinade. Grill, brushing occasionally with marinade, for 10 minutes or until pale golden and cooked through.
4 Serve on a bed of stir-fried peppers, broccoli, courgettes and sugar snap peas sprinkled with light soy sauce, with extra satay sauce.

TIME: *preparation 30 minutes; marinating 1 hour; cooking 10 minutes*
NUTRIENTS PER SERVING: *Calories 130; Total fat 5 g; Fibre 0 g; Carbohydrate 2 g*

FOOD EDITOR'S TIP

To save time preparing vegetable accompaniments, use a packet of ready-chopped stir-fry vegetables.

Peppered meatloaf

- 1 onion, finely chopped
- 1 lb (450 g) fresh minced beef
- 2 garlic cloves, crushed
- 2 oz (50 g) white breadcrumbs
- 1 tablespoon dried mixed herbs
- 1 tablespoon tomato purée
- 2 eggs (size 3), beaten
- 2 teaspoons mixed peppercorns, coarsely ground

1 Put onion into a large bowl with minced beef, garlic, breadcrumbs, herbs, tomato purée, eggs and peppercorns. Stir until thoroughly mixed. Season well.

2 Spoon into a greased and base-lined 1 lb (450 g) loaf tin. Cover tin tightly with foil. Cook at 350°F (180°C), Gas 4 for 1½ hours.

3 Remove from oven and leave to stand for 5 minutes. Serve in thick slices with onion gravy, buttered tagliatelle, grilled tomatoes with parsley and sautéd red pepper and onions. Garnish with mixed salad leaves.

TIME: *preparation 10 minutes; cooking 1½ hours; standing 5 minutes*
NUTRIENTS PER SERVING: *Calories 230; Total fat 9 g; Fibre 1 g; Carbohydrate 10 g*

FOOD EDITOR'S TIP

Use fresh mince if you plan to cook ahead and freeze this dish.

Scrambled jacket potatoes

- 4 x 6 oz (150 g) baking potatoes
- 8 oz (225 g) low-fat sausages
- 2 oz (50 g) button mushrooms, quartered
- 4 eggs (size 3), beaten
- 5 tablespoons skimmed milk

1 Prick potatoes with a fork and cook at 400°F (200°C), Gas 6 for 1 hour or until tender.

2 Cook sausages and quartered mushrooms under grill. Cut up the cooked sausages into bite-sized pieces.

3 Whisk eggs and milk together. Cook, stirring over a low heat, for 5 minutes until lightly set. Stir in sausages and mushrooms. Keep hot.

4 Cut a deep cross in the jacket potatoes. Place on individual serving plates and spoon the scrambled egg and sausage mixture into cut centre and around the potatoes. Serve with cherry tomatoes.

TIME: *preparation 5 minutes; cooking 1 hour*
NUTRIENTS PER SERVING: *Calories 370; Total fat 19 g; Fibre 3 g; Carbohydrate 33 g*

FOOD EDITOR'S TIP

Threading metal skewers through the potatoes before baking will reduce the cooking time by about 20 minutes.

Pork schnitzel

- 4 x 4 oz (100 g) pork chops, boned
- 3 oz (75 g) fresh white breadcrumbs
- 1 oz (25 g) plain flour
- 1 egg (size 3), beaten
- 5 fl oz (142 ml) single cream
- 1 teaspoon mustard powder
- 1 oz (25 g) gherkins, finely chopped
- ½ oz (15 g) capers, halved

1 Put pork chops between two sheets of greaseproof paper and beat with a rolling pin until chops are flattened to twice their original size. Season breadcrumbs well.

2 Put flour, beaten egg and breadcrumbs into three bowls. Dip chops into flour first, then egg, then breadcrumbs to coat well. Grill chops for 12 minutes, turning once, until crisp.

3 Meanwhile, gently heat cream with mustard powder, gherkins and capers. Season.

4 Drizzle cream sauce over pork chops, and serve accompanied by steamed carrots, broccoli and stir-fried vegetable rice. Garnish dish with mustard and cress and lemon wedges.

TIME: *preparation 10 minutes; cooking 12 minutes*
NUTRIENTS PER SERVING: *Calories 300; Total fat 15 g; Fibre 1 g; Carbohydrate 15 g*

FOOD EDITOR'S TIP

Bread that is a day old makes finer breadcrumbs than very fresh bread.

Sausages 'n' beans

- 1 lb (450 g) baking potatoes, thinly sliced
- 12 oz (325 g) packet reduced-fat pork sausages
- 15 oz (425 g) can mixed beans
- 8.1 oz (230 g) can tomatoes with herbs

1 Put potato slices into a saucepan. Cover with cold water and bring to boil. Drain and arrange in a single layer on a lightly greased baking sheet. Cook at 425°F (220°C), Gas 7 for 30 minutes or until golden.

2 Meanwhile, grill sausages, turning occasionally, for 8–10 minutes or until lightly browned. Cut each sausage diagonally into three pieces. Put sausages, mixed beans and tomatoes into a saucepan. Bring to boil. Cover and simmer for 5 minutes.

3 Serve with blanched spring onions and green cabbage, mangetout or green beans.

TIME: *preparation 15 minutes; cooking 30 minutes*
NUTRIENTS PER SERVING: *Calories 340; Total fat 12 g; Fibre 7 g; Carbohydrate 45 g*

FOOD EDITOR'S TIP

Sprinkle potato slices with a little cayenne pepper for a hot spicy flavour.

Cheesy bacon slice

- 2 tablespoons olive oil
- 4 oz (100 g) rindless smoked back bacon, chopped
- 4 oz (100 g) button mushrooms, sliced
- ½ bunch spring onions, finely chopped
- 6 eggs (size 3)
- 4 oz (100 g) mature cheddar, grated
- 2 tablespoons chopped fresh parsley

1. Heat olive oil in a large frying pan. Fry bacon, mushrooms and spring onions for 2-3 minutes until tender.
2. In a large jug, beat together eggs and cheddar with parsley and season with freshly ground black pepper.
3. Pour egg mixture into frying pan over bacon and mushrooms and cook over a medium heat for 5 minutes or until underside of egg mixture is golden.
4. Put pan under a preheated grill and cook for a further 5 minutes or until top is set and bubbling. Cut into four wedges and serve with a jacket potato, green beans and salad leaves.

TIME: *preparation 10 minutes; cooking 13 minutes*
NUTRIENTS PER SERVING: *Calories 300; Total fat 19 g; Fibre 3 g; Carbohydrate 9 g*

FOOD EDITOR'S TIP

Use unsmoked bacon for a less salty flavour.

Herb crust cutlets

- 2 oz (50 g) Granary breadcrumbs
- 1 oz (25 g) toasted hazelnuts
- 2 tablespoons each fresh parsley and thyme
- 1 teaspoon olive oil
- 1 garlic clove, crushed
- 8 x 3 oz (75 g) lamb cutlets
- 2 tablespoons orange juice
- 6 tablespoons red wine
- 3 tablespoons redcurrant jelly
- 1 teaspoon arrowroot

1. Process breadcrumbs, hazelnuts, parsley and thyme for 1 minute. Add oil, garlic and seasoning. Blend 2 minutes.
2. Trim cutlets and cover each with herb mixture. Put on a rack over a roasting tin. Cook at 375°F (190°C), Gas 5 for 20 minutes.
3. Meanwhile, gently heat orange juice, wine and jelly for 3 minutes. Mix arrowroot with 2 tablespoons water to form a paste. Add to pan. Stir sauce over a low heat until it thickens slightly and becomes clear. Simmer for 2 minutes.
4. Serve cutlets with sauce, sautéd potatoes and steamed vegetables. Garnish with thyme.

TIME: *preparation 20 minutes; cooking 20 minutes*
NUTRIENTS PER SERVING: *Calories 240; Total fat 11 g; Fibre 4 g; Carbohydrate 6 g*

FOOD EDITOR'S TIP

If you like your lamb well done, cook for an extra 10 minutes.

Lamb hotpot

- 1 lb (450 g) frozen diced lamb, thawed
- 1 head celery
- 2 leeks, washed and sliced
- 1 lb (450 g) carrots, peeled and cut into sticks
- 14 oz (397 g) can tomatoes
- 2 tablespoons tomato purée
- 1 teaspoon dried rosemary
- 5 fl oz (142 ml) lamb stock
- 2 teaspoons cornflour
- 1½ lb (675 g) potatoes, thinly sliced

1 Trim fat from lamb. Dry-fry in a nonstick frying pan for 5 minutes or until browned. Chop celery and add to pan with leeks and carrots. Cook for 10 minutes, stirring occasionally, until just softened.

2 Stir in tomatoes, tomato purée, rosemary, stock and seasoning. Bring to boil. Spoon into a 3 pint (1.7 litre) ovenproof dish. Cover with a lid or foil and cook at 325°F (160°C), Gas 3 for 1½ hours.

3 Increase oven temperature to 400°F (200°C), Gas 6. Mix cornflour with 2 tablespoons cold water to form a smooth paste. Stir paste into lamb mixture to thicken sauce.

4 Arrange potato slices, overlapping, on top of lamb. Cover with oiled foil and cook for 30 minutes. Uncover and cook for a further 30 minutes until potatoes are tender. Serve with extra steamed carrots and leeks and garnish with a sprig of fresh rosemary.

TIME: *preparation 20 minutes; cooking 2¾ hours*
NUTRIENTS PER SERVING: *Calories 350; Total fat 10 g; Fibre 7 g; Carbohydrate 42 g*

FOOD EDITOR'S TIP

If you prefer, replace the celery with 8 oz (225 g) sliced button mushrooms.

Chow mein

- 9 oz (250 g) packet medium egg noodles
- 2 tablespoons sunflower oil
- 2 oz (50 g) cooked chicken breast, cut into strips
- 3 oz (75 g) cooked ham, cut into strips
- 3 oz (75 g) mangetout, trimmed
- 1 red pepper, halved, deseeded and cut into strips
- 4 oz (100 g) beansprouts
- 2 spring onions, thinly sliced
- 2 tablespoons soy sauce
- 1 tablespoon chilli and garlic sauce

1 Soak noodles in boiling water with 1 teaspoon oil for 6 minutes, or according to packet instructions.

2 Meanwhile, heat remaining oil in a wok or large frying pan. Add cooked chicken, ham, mangetout, pepper and beansprouts and stir-fry for 2 minutes. Remove with a slotted spoon and keep hot. Drain noodles.

3 Add spring onions and noodles to wok or pan and cook for 1 minute. Add soy sauce and chilli and garlic sauce. Cook for 2 minutes until hot. Season.

4 Spoon noodles into individual serving bowls and arrange stir-fry on top.

TIME: *preparation 20 minutes; soaking 6 minutes; cooking 5 minutes*
NUTRIENTS PER SERVING: *Calories 370; Total fat 13 g; Fibre 3 g; Carbohydrate 49 g*

FOOD EDITOR'S TIP

Very quick and easy to prepare, this is a great way to use up leftover cooked chicken.

Salad niçoise

- ½ iceberg lettuce
- 4 oz (100 g) cherry tomatoes
- 3 eggs (size 3), hard-boiled, shelled and quartered
- 12 black olives, pitted
- 4 oz (100 g) cooked French beans, trimmed
- 2 shallots, thinly sliced
- 14.1 oz (400 g) can tuna in brine, drained and flaked
- 2 teaspoons red wine vinegar
- 2 tablespoons sunflower oil
- 1 garlic clove, crushed
- 1 tablespoon chopped fresh parsley
- 1 teaspoon freshly ground black pepper

1 Tear lettuce leaves and arrange on a large serving platter. Halve cherry tomatoes and arrange over lettuce with eggs, olives, French beans, shallots and flaked tuna.
2 In a bowl, whisk together vinegar, sunflower oil, garlic and chopped parsley. Season well with freshly ground black pepper.
3 Drizzle vinaigrette dressing over salad. Serve with warm crusty bread.

TIME: *preparation 5 minutes*
NUTRIENTS PER SERVING: *Calories 315; Total fat 22 g; Fibre 3 g; Carbohydrate 3 g*

FOOD EDITOR'S TIP
You'll find sunflower oil makes a much lighter dressing than olive oil.

Trawlerman's pie

- 3 x 6 oz (150 g) baking potatoes
- 10 fl oz (284 ml) vegetable stock
- 10 fl oz (284 ml) tomato sauce
- 2 x 11 oz (300 g) packets cod steaks, thawed and cubed
- 1 oz (25 g) parmesan, grated
- 1 tablespoon chopped fresh parsley, or 1 teaspoon dried

1 Prick potatoes with a fork and cook at 400°F (200°C), Gas 6 for 1 hour or until tender. Slice.
2 Stir stock and tomato sauce in a saucepan. Cook over low heat for 5 minutes. Season.
3 Stir cubed cod steaks into sauce. Season well, cover and cook over low heat for 5 minutes.
4 Spoon mixture into four 10 fl oz (284 ml) ovenproof dishes. Arrange potatoes on top. Cook at 400°F (200°C), Gas 6 for 25 minutes.
5 Mix parmesan and parsley together. Sprinkle over potatoes. Serve with baby carrots and French beans.

TIME: *preparation 25 minutes; cooking 1 hour 25 minutes*
NUTRIENTS PER SERVING: *Calories 280; Total fat 7 g; Fibre 2 g; Carbohydrate 25 g*

FOOD EDITOR'S TIP
You could substitute white sauce for the tomato as an alternative.

Pepper fish parcels

- 4 x 6 oz (150 g) hoki fillets, washed and dried
- 1 each red and green pepper, deseeded and cut into rings
- 1 small onion, sliced into rings
- 2 oz (50 g) button mushrooms, sliced
- 8 black olives
- 1 small lemon

1. Cut out four 9 inch (23 cm) squares of foil and oil the dull side lightly. Place a hoki fillet in the centre of each square and season well.
2. Arrange pepper and onion rings, mushrooms and olives on the top of each fillet. Halve lemon and squeeze juice from one half over fillets, reserving the remaining half.
3. Bring edges of foil together to form a parcel and twist to seal tightly. Place parcels on to a baking sheet and cook at 400°F (200°C), Gas 6 for 15-20 minutes, or until fish flakes easily.
4. Unwrap parcels and put on a plate. Spoon juices over, serve with broccoli and new potatoes. Garnish with remaining lemon and parsley.

TIME: *preparation 25 minutes; cooking 20 minutes*
NUTRIENTS PER SERVING: *Calories 175; Total fat 3 g; Fibre 3 g; Carbohydrate 6 g*

FOOD EDITOR'S TIP

Make sure to cut the peppers and onions thinly so they will cook in the same time as the fish.

Creamy fish bake

- ½ x 14 oz (400 g) can ratatouille
- 4 x 3¼ oz (92 g) frozen cod portions, thawed
- 13 oz (376 g) can white wine and cream sauce
- 3 oz (75 g) Granary bread
- 4 oz (100 g) cheddar, grated
- 1 tablespoon chopped fresh parsley

1. Divide ratatouille between four 10 fl oz (284 ml) individual ovenproof dishes. Place a cod portion on top of the ratatouille.
2. Spoon white wine and cream sauce over fish, ensuring fish is completely covered.
3. Remove crusts from bread. Put bread in a blender or food processor for 1 minute to form breadcrumbs. Stir in grated cheese, chopped parsley and seasoning. Sprinkle breadcrumb mixture over sauce.
4. Place dishes on a baking sheet. Cook at 350°F (180°C), Gas 4 for 25 minutes or until fish is tender. Garnish with parsley and lemon, serve with salad leaves, spring onions and tomatoes.

TIME: *preparation 15 minutes; cooking 25 minutes*
NUTRIENTS PER SERVING: *Calories 260; Total fat 10 g; Fibre 2 g; Carbohydrate 19 g*

FOOD EDITOR'S TIP

For special occasions add prawns or other shellfish to this dish.

LOW IN CALORIES

Cheesy baked fish

- 4 oz (100 g) reduced-fat cheddar, grated
- 2 teaspoons wholegrain mustard
- 3 tablespoons skimmed milk
- 4 x 3 oz (75 g) plaice fillets, skinned
- 1 lb (450 g) tomatoes
- 1 small fennel bulb
- ½ bunch spring onions

1 Mix together cheddar, mustard and milk to a thick paste. Put plaice fillets, skinned side up, on a board and spread one-quarter of the cheese mixture over each.
2 Roll up each from the widest end and secure with a cocktail stick. Put on a baking sheet and grill for 10 minutes.
3 Meanwhile, finely chop tomatoes and fennel and put into a saucepan. Bring to boil and simmer for 5 minutes. Finely slice spring onions, add to tomato and fennel and cook for 5 minutes or until fennel and onions are softened and sauce thickened slightly.
4 Serve plaice with tomato and fennel sauce and mixed vegetable rice and peas, garnished with fennel fronds and lemon wedges.

TIME: *preparation 15 minutes; cooking 10 minutes*
NUTRIENTS PER SERVING: *Calories 170; Total fat 6 g; Fibre 3 g; Carbohydrate 5 g*

FOOD EDITOR'S TIP

If fennel is hard to find, use dried mixed herbs in the sauce instead.

Haddock creole

- 2 tablespoons olive oil
- 1 each small red, yellow and green pepper, deseeded and cut into strips
- 1 onion, sliced
- 2 garlic cloves, crushed
- 14 oz (397 g) can chopped tomatoes
- 1 lemon, grated rind and juice
- 2 x 11 oz (300 g) packets frozen haddock fillets

1 Heat oil in a large saucepan. Add all peppers, onion and garlic. Fry for 3 minutes until softened.
2 Stir in tomatoes, lemon rind and half the juice. Add haddock, season and bring to the boil. Cover and simmer for 6 minutes.
3 Turn fish over and cook for 6 minutes or until flesh flakes easily when pressed with a knife.
4 Serve fish with long grain rice, garnished with lemon and parsley.

TIME: *preparation 15 minutes; cooking 16 minutes*
NUTRIENTS PER SERVING: *Calories 220; Total fat 8 g; Fibre 3 g; Carbohydrate 10 g*

FOOD EDITOR'S TIP

If you find the tomato and lemon juice a little too acidic, add approximately ¼ teaspoon sugar.

Tuna and sweetcorn pizza

- 8 oz (225 g) strong plain flour
- ½ teaspoon salt
- ½ oz (15 g) butter
- ¼ oz (5 g) sachet easy-blend dried yeast
- 6 fl oz (170 ml) hand-hot water
- 1 onion, finely sliced
- 1 garlic clove, crushed
- 1 tablespoon sunflower oil
- 1 tablespoon tomato purée
- 14 oz (397 g) can chopped tomatoes
- 4 oz (100 g) baby corn cobs
- 6½ oz (185 g) can tuna in brine, drained
- 3 oz (75 g) half-fat cheddar, grated

1 Put flour and salt into a bowl. Rub in butter to form fine breadcrumbs. Stir in yeast.
2 Add enough hand-hot water to form a soft dough.
3 Knead dough until smooth. Roll out to fit a 10 inch (25 cm) round pizza tin. Prick base and cook at 425°F (220°C), Gas 7 for 5 minutes.
4 Put onions, garlic and oil into a saucepan and cook for 2 minutes. Stir in tomato purée and tomatoes. Season and cook for 15 minutes.
5 Spoon over base. Put corn cobs and tuna on top. Sprinkle on the grated cheese.
6 Cook at 425°F (220°C), Gas 7 for 20-25 minutes. Serve with a mixed leaf salad.

TIME: *preparation 30 minutes; cooking 47 minutes*
NUTRIENTS PER SERVING: *Calories 380; Total fat 11 g; Fibre 4 g; Carbohydrate 50 g*

FOOD EDITOR'S TIP

If you prefer, use sweetcorn niblets instead of baby corn cobs.

Trout and herb rolls

- 7 oz (200 g) low-fat soft cheese
- 1 tablespoon chopped fresh tarragon
- 2 tablespoons snipped fresh chives
- 8 x 3 oz (75 g) skinless trout fillets
- 5 oz (125 g) Greek strained yogurt
- 1 tablespoon lemon juice

1 Mix together low-fat soft cheese, tarragon and 1 tablespoon chives. Season well. Lay trout fillets out flat and spread the cheese and herb mixture over.
2 Starting at the thick end of each fillet, roll up and secure with a cocktail stick.
3 Put fish rolls on a plate over a pan of simmering water and steam for 10-15 minutes or until tender. Meanwhile, mix together yogurt and remaining chives, reserving some for garnish. Add lemon juice and seasoning. Sprinkle over chives before serving.
4 Serve trout with yogurt dressing, lemon wedges and a mixed leaf salad.

TIME: *preparation 15 minutes; cooking 15 minutes*
NUTRIENTS PER SERVING: *Calories 250; Total fat 9 g; Fibre 0 g; Carbohydrate 2 g*

FOOD EDITOR'S TIP

Use plaice instead of trout for a more economical dish.

Spring parcels

- 1 large onion, chopped
- 1 garlic clove, crushed
- 14 oz (397 g) can tomatoes
- 1½ tablespoons tomato purée
- ½ tablespoon paprika
- 6 oz (150 g) long grain rice
- 8 savoy cabbage leaves
- 1 red pepper, finely sliced
- 3 spring onions, finely sliced
- 2 oz (50 g) button mushrooms, sliced
- 1 tablespoon fresh mixed herbs
- 4 oz (100 g) edam, cubed
- 1 carrot, grated

1 Dry-fry onion and garlic for 5 minutes in a nonstick pan. Add tomatoes, purée and paprika. Cook for 20 minutes.

2 Meanwhile, boil rice for 15 minutes or according to packet instructions. Drain. Remove core from cabbage leaves and discard. Steam leaves for 5 minutes until just tender. Drain on kitchen paper.

3 Mix together rice, red pepper, spring onions, mushrooms and herbs. Season well.

4 Spoon rice on to each cabbage leaf. Top each leaf with a few cubes of cheese. Fold and roll up to form parcels. Steam for 10 minutes.

5 Meanwhile, bring tomato sauce to boil. Add carrot and simmer for 8 minutes. Serve parcels with tomato sauce and garnish with grated lemon rind.

TIME: *preparation 25 minutes; cooking 38 minutes*
NUTRIENTS PER SERVING: *Calories 230; Total fat 8 g; Fibre 3 g; Carbohydrate 29 g*

FOOD EDITOR'S TIP

Large cabbage leaves are best for making these parcels.

Vegetable tortilla

- 8 oz (225 g) courgettes, sliced
- 2 sticks celery, sliced
- 4 oz (100 g) carrots, diced
- 8 oz (225 g) potatoes, diced
- 4 oz (100 g) baby sweetcorn, halved
- 1 garlic clove, crushed
- 14 oz (397 g) can tomatoes
- 2 tablespoons tomato purée
- 1 teaspoon ground coriander
- 1 teaspoon ground cumin
- 5 fl oz (142 ml) vegetable stock
- 10.2 oz (290 g) packet pizza base mix

1 Put all ingredients except pizza mix into a large pan. Simmer for 20 minutes, stirring.

2 Meanwhile, make up pizza base according to packet instructions. Knead dough for 5 minutes or until smooth. Divide into four pieces.

3 Roll out each piece to a 7 inch (18 cm) circle. Put on a baking sheet. Grill for 5 minutes each side. Repeat with remainder. Put on serving plates.

4 Spoon vegetables on to tortillas. Garnish with yogurt, red chilli and flat leaf parsley. Serve with salad.

TIME: *preparation 25 minutes; cooking 20 minutes*
NUTRIENTS PER SERVING: *Calories 330; Total fat 4 g; Fibre 3 g; Carbohydrate 65 g*

FOOD EDITOR'S TIP

If you like spicy, hot food stir some chopped chilli into the vegetables.

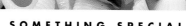

SOMETHING SPECIAL

Chicken chilli with rice

- 4 x 4 oz (100 g) boneless, skinless chicken breasts, thickly sliced
- 1 tablespoon oil
- 1 onion, roughly chopped
- 1 green pepper, deseeded and roughly chopped
- 14 oz (397 g) can chopped tomatoes
- ½ teaspoon hot chilli powder
- 3 tablespoons tomato purée
- 12 oz (325 g) basmati rice
- 14 oz (397 g) can red kidney beans, drained

1 Stir-fry chicken in oil in a large saucepan for 5 minutes. Add chopped onion and green pepper. Cook for 5 minutes.
2 Stir in chopped tomatoes, chilli powder and tomato purée. Season well, cover with lid and cook for 20 minutes.
3 Meanwhile, cook basmati rice according to packet instructions.
4 Stir kidney beans into chilli mixture and cook for a further 10 minutes, uncovered.
5 Drain basmati rice and spoon on to individual serving plates with chicken. Garnish with a sprig of fresh coriander.

TIME: *preparation 20 minutes; cooking 40 minutes*
NUTRIENTS PER SERVING: *Calories 670; Total fat 10 g; Fibre 20 g; Carbohydrate 105 g*

FOOD EDITOR'S TIP

Choose your chilli powder carefully as some are hotter than others.

Chicken tikka kebabs with rice

- 6 tablespoons chicken tikka paste
- 5 oz (125 g) carton natural yogurt
- 1 lb (450 g) boneless, skinless chicken breasts, cubed
- 8 oz (225 g) long grain rice
- pinch of turmeric
- ½ cucumber, cut into thin sticks

1 Mix the tikka paste with 4 tablespoons yogurt. Stir in cubed chicken, cover dish and leave to marinate in the fridge for 30 minutes.
2 Cook rice and turmeric in salted boiling water for 15 minutes or until just tender.
3 Meanwhile, thread chicken pieces on to eight wooden skewers. Grill for 15 minutes, turning the chicken occasionally.
4 Make cucumber and yogurt dip by mixing the cucumber with remaining yogurt. Spoon into a small bowl. Cover and chill until required.
5 Drain rice and divide between four warmed plates and lay two chicken kebabs on top of each. Serve accompanied by yogurt dip and naan bread. Garnish with sprigs of fresh coriander and lemon wedges.

TIME: *preparation 15 minutes; marinating 30 minutes; cooking 15 minutes*
NUTRIENTS PER SERVING: *Calories 420; Total fat 24 g; Fibre 2 g; Carbohydrate 27 g*

FOOD EDITOR'S TIP

The most economical way of buying chicken is to buy it whole and joint it yourself. The carcass can be used afterwards for making soup.

Chicken roulé

- 4 x 6 oz (150 g) boneless, skinless chicken breasts
- 6 oz (150 g) button mushrooms
- 6 oz (150 g) packet coarse farmhouse pâté
- 3 oz (75 g) butter
- 4 oz (100 g) shiitake mushrooms, halved
- 2 onions, thinly sliced
- 1 pint (568 ml) vegetable stock
- 3 oz (75 g) ready-to-eat dried apricots

1 Beat chicken breasts separately in a polybag with a rolling pin until ¼ inch (6 mm) thick.
2 Finely chop 2 oz (50 g) button mushrooms and stir into pâté. Divide pâté into four and spread to within ½ inch (1.3 cm) of edge of chicken breasts. Roll up lengthways.
3 Tightly wrap each breast in a square of buttered foil. Put on a baking sheet, cook at 400°F (200°C), Gas 6 for 20 minutes.
4 Meanwhile, cut remaining button mushrooms in half. Melt 2 oz (50 g) butter in a frying pan. Add the halved mushrooms and the onion, and cook for 5 minutes. Stir in stock and apricots and simmer until stock is reduced by half.
5 Remove mushrooms and apricots with a slotted spoon, spoon on to serving plates and keep hot. Add remaining butter to pan and whisk sauce over a low heat until thickened.
6 Unwrap chicken and cut each breast into five slices. Arrange on top of mushroom mixture. Drizzle sauce over. Serve with new potatoes, steamed carrots and courgettes.

TIME: *preparation 40 minutes; cooking 20 minutes*
NUTRIENTS PER SERVING: *Calories 500; Total fat 32 g; Fibre 12 g; Carbohydrate 14 g*

FOOD EDITOR'S TIP

If you can't get shiitake mushrooms, use a different type such as brown cap.

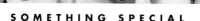

Garlic chicken

- 4 x 6 oz (150 g) part-boned chicken breasts
- 2 x 2¾ oz (70 g) packets garlic and herb cream cheese

1 Remove skin from chicken pieces. Cut four slits in each breast.
2 Divide each cheese into eight. Insert pieces into chicken slits. Put in roasting tin. Chill for 15 minutes.
3 Cook chicken at 400°F (200°C), Gas 6 for 35 minutes or until juices run clear when meat is pierced.
4 Serve with creamy mashed potato swirls, carrots and greens. Garnish each plate with a few fresh coriander leaves.

TIME: *preparation 30 minutes; chilling 15 minutes; cooking 35 minutes*
NUTRIENTS PER SERVING: *Calories 300; Total fat 22 g; Fibre 0 g; Carbohydrate 0 g*

FOOD EDITOR'S TIP

To make potato swirls for a special occasion, make mash extra creamy with butter and milk. Spoon into a piping bag fitted with a star nozzle. Pipe on to a greased tray and reheat in the oven.

Coconut chicken

- 2 lb (900 g) bag frozen, part-boned chicken breasts, thawed
- 2 tablespoons sunflower oil
- 1 onion, finely chopped
- 2 garlic cloves, crushed
- ½ x 6½ oz (190 g) jar Malaysian curry paste
- 8 oz (225 g) long grain rice
- pinch of salt
- ½ oz (15 g) desiccated coconut

1 Remove skin and bones from chicken breasts. Cut flesh into bite-sized pieces.
2 Using a large frying pan, stir-fry chicken pieces in oil in two batches for 6-7 minutes or until browned.
3 Add onion and garlic to pan, fry until softened. Add curry paste with 10 fl oz (284 ml) water. Bring mixture to boil, then reduce heat, cover and simmer for 10 minutes. Uncover and simmer for a further 10 minutes or until chicken is tender.
4 Meanwhile, rinse long grain rice and put into a large saucepan with 1 pint (568 ml) water and a pinch of salt. Bring to boil, cover and simmer for 15 minutes or until tender. Drain.
5 Mix desiccated coconut into rice and spoon into four teacups. Press down well.
6 Turn out each rice mould on to a serving plate and spoon chicken round it. Serve garnished with toasted coconut, fresh coriander leaves, chopped red chilli and spring onion.

TIME: *preparation 30 minutes; cooking 34 minutes*
NUTRIENTS PER SERVING: *Calories 850; Total fat 44 g; Fibre 1 g; Carbohydrate 70 g*

FOOD EDITOR'S TIP

You don't need as much oil if you stir-fry the chicken in a nonstick pan.

Lemon chicken

- 4 x 6 oz (150 g) boneless, skinless chicken breasts, scored
- 1 lemon, zest and juice
- 2¾ oz (70 g) packet garlic butter, melted

1 Put chicken breasts on grill pan. Mix lemon zest, juice and garlic butter together. Brush evenly over chicken.

2 Grill chicken for 15 minutes until juices run clear, turn twice and baste with garlic butter mixture while cooking.

3 Serve with broccoli, boiled new potatoes tossed in butter, chopped parsley and rock salt, and baby carrots tossed in honey, garnished with lemon wedges.

TIME: *preparation 10 minutes; cooking 15 minutes*
NUTRIENTS PER SERVING: *Calories 280; Total fat 20 g; Fibre 0 g; Carbohydrate Trace*

FOOD EDITOR'S TIP

Look for frozen chicken breasts which are always cheaper than fresh.

Thai chicken and noodles

- 1 oz (25 g) desiccated coconut
- 6 fl oz (150 ml) boiling water
- 1 onion, quartered
- 2 garlic cloves
- 1 lemon, rind only
- 1 tablespoon light olive oil
- ¼ teaspoon hot chilli powder
- ¼ teaspoon ground ginger
- 2 tablespoons dark soy sauce
- 4 tablespoons crunchy peanut butter
- 4 x 6 oz (150 g) boneless, skinless chicken breasts
- 9 oz (250 g) packet egg noodles
- 5 fl oz (142 ml) chicken stock
- 4 oz (100 g) mangetout, finely shredded

1 Soak coconut in boiling water. Combine onion, garlic, lemon rind, oil, chilli powder, salt, ginger and soy sauce in food processor until smooth. Drain coconut. Add to processor with peanut butter.

2 Cut three deep slashes in chicken. Put in shallow dish with peanut mixture. Marinate overnight.

3 Remove chicken, reserving marinade. Cook under preheated grill for 15 minutes. Cook noodles as packet instructions.

4 Stir marinade and stock over low heat until mixture boils.

5 Steam mangetout. Drain noodles, add mangetout. Put noodles with chicken on plates. Drizzle over peanut sauce. Garnish with coriander leaves.

TIME: *preparation 20 minutes; marinating overnight; cooking 26 minutes*
NUTRIENTS PER SERVING: *Calories 480; Total fat 21 g; Fibre 4 g; Carbohydrate 33 g*

FOOD EDITOR'S TIP

If you don't have a processor, chop the onion and garlic by hand until very fine, then stir in remaining ingredients.

Chicken korma

- 2 tablespoons ground coriander
- 1 tablespoon ground cumin
- 1 tablespoon desiccated coconut
- 2 oz (50 g) cashew nuts
- 1 large onion, roughly chopped
- 3 garlic cloves, peeled
- 1½ inch (3.8 cm) piece root ginger, peeled
- 1 large tomato, peeled
- 1 teaspoon ground turmeric
- 4 tablespoons vegetable oil
- 6 each cardamom pods, whole cloves and black peppercorns
- 1 bay leaf
- 1 dried red chilli
- 4 x 6 oz (150 g) boneless, skinless chicken breasts
- 1 tablespoon natural yogurt
- 1 teaspoon salt

1 Put coriander, cumin, coconut and cashew nuts into a nonstick frying pan. Cook for 2-3 minutes. Remove from pan and set aside.
2 Blend onion, garlic, ginger, tomato and turmeric in a food processor for 1 minute to form a smooth paste.
3 Heat 2 tablespoons oil in frying pan, add cardamom pods, cloves, peppercorns, bay leaf and chilli. Cook for 3 minutes. Reduce heat, add chicken in two batches. Fry each batch for 5 minutes.
4 Remove chicken. Add onion paste and remaining oil. Cook, stirring, for 5 minutes. Add spice mixture, cook for 5 minutes. Stir in yogurt and salt.
5 Return chicken to pan with enough water to cover. Cook, stirring occasionally, for 1 hour. Serve with rice, spinach leaves and sliced tomatoes. Garnish with coriander.

TIME: *preparation 30 minutes; cooking 1 hour 26 minutes*
NUTRIENTS PER SERVING: *Calories 440; Total fat 27 g; Fibre 1 g; Carbohydrate 8 g*

FOOD EDITOR'S TIP

Cook rice, don't rinse and pack into oiled timbales or tea cups, and then turn out.

Teriyaki chicken and rice

- 4 chicken quarters
- 8 fl oz (227 ml) teriyaki marinade
- 2 tablespoons clear honey
- 1 orange, grated rind and juice
- 8 oz (225 g) basmati rice
- 2 carrots, cut into julienne strips
- 1 courgette, cut into julienne strips
- 1 teaspoon cornflour

1 Skin chicken quarters and make deep slashes in each. Put chicken into a roasting tin.
2 Mix together teriyaki marinade, honey, orange rind and juice. Pour over chicken. Leave to marinate for 30 minutes.
3 Drain marinade, reserve. Cook chicken at 425°F (220°C), Gas 7 for 10 minutes. Reduce heat to 375°F (190°C), Gas 5, cook for 40 minutes or until juices run clear when pierced with a skewer.
4 Meanwhile, boil rice for 8 minutes. Boil carrot and courgette juliennes for 2 minutes. Drain, toss with rice.
5 Mix together reserved marinade, cornflour and 4 fl oz (114 ml) water. Stir over a low heat until thickened. Spoon a little sauce over chicken. Serve with rice, garnish with parsley.

TIME: *preparation 15 minutes; marinating 30 minutes; cooking 50 minutes*
NUTRIENTS PER SERVING: *Calories 430; Total fat 7 g; Fibre 2 g; Carbohydrate 59 g*

FOOD EDITOR'S TIP

You should find teriyaki marinade with the other condiments such as soy sauce and Worcestershire sauce at your supermarket.

Steak Diane

- 4 x 5 oz (125 g) fillet steaks
- 2 tablespoons olive oil
- 1 oz (25 g) butter
- 5 fl oz (142 ml) beef stock
- 2 tablespoons Worcestershire sauce
- 10 fl oz (284 ml) double cream
- 2 tablespoons brandy

1 Using a sharp knife, carefully trim fat from steaks. Heat olive oil and butter in a large, heavy-based frying pan. Cook steaks two at a time for 3 minutes each side or until tender. Put on a serving plate and keep hot.

2 Add stock to frying pan and boil, stirring occasionally, until reduced to approximately 2 tablespoons. Stir in Worcestershire sauce and cream, scraping off sediment from base of pan. Stir until heated through. Add brandy and seasoning.

3 Serve steaks and cream sauce with straw chips, asparagus tips, carrots and cauliflower.

TIME: *preparation 20 minutes; cooking 14 minutes*
NUTRIENTS PER SERVING: *Calories 600; Total fat 51 g; Fibre 0 g; Carbohydrate 2 g*

FOOD EDITOR'S TIP

If serving with chips, heat oil and cook chips until almost cooked. Drain, cook steaks and reheat chips in oil when steaks are ready.

Duck à l'orange

- 4 x 6 oz (150 g) duck breasts
- 2 tablespoons clear honey
- 1 tablespoon red wine vinegar
- 2 tablespoons port
- 1 orange, juice and rind
- 1 tablespoon redcurrant jelly
- 1 tablespoon arrowroot

1 Put duck breasts, skin side up and a little spaced apart, into a roasting tin. Brush with honey. Cook at 400°F (200°C), Gas 6 for 20 minutes, baste with honey and juices then cook for a further 10 minutes.

2 Meanwhile, put red wine vinegar, port, orange juice and rind and redcurrant jelly in a small saucepan. Bring to boil and simmer for 15 minutes, stirring until thickened.

3 Remove duck from oven. Slice and put on to serving plates. Keep hot. Pour duck juices into sauce. Mix together arrowroot and enough water to make a smooth paste. Stir into saucepan and simmer for 2 minutes until thickened. Serve duck with boiled new potatoes, drained and fried in butter, sauce, mangetout and baby sweetcorn. Garnish with orange segments.

TIME: *preparation 20 minutes; cooking 32 minutes*
NUTRIENTS PER SERVING: *Calories 480; Total fat 36 g; Fibre 0 g; Carbohydrate 13 g*

FOOD EDITOR'S TIP

For a non-alcoholic sauce, replace the port with an equal amount of orange juice.

Steak and tomato concassée

- 3 tablespoons olive oil
- 4 x 6 oz (150 g) sirloin steaks
- 2 onions, finely chopped
- 2 garlic cloves, crushed
- 1 lb (450 g) tomatoes, skinned, deseeded and chopped
- 1 lb (450 g) courgettes, diced
- 2 tablespoons chopped fresh basil
- 5 fl oz (142 ml) white wine
- 3 teaspoons caster sugar

1 Heat 2 tablespoons oil in a frying pan. Cook steaks for 8 minutes, turning once. Remove steaks and set aside.

2 Add remaining oil, onions and garlic to pan, cook for 4 minutes.

3 Stir in tomatoes, courgettes, fresh basil, white wine and sugar. Cover and simmer for 10 minutes.

4 Uncover, place steaks on top. Cook for a further 10 minutes. Serve sprinkled with grated parmesan.

TIME: *preparation 20 minutes; cooking 40 minutes*
NUTRIENTS PER SERVING: *Calories 630; Total fat 48 g; Fibre 2 g; Carbohydrate 15 g*

FOOD EDITOR'S TIP

Very ripe tomatoes are particularly suitable for this dish.

Beef olives

- 2 oz (50 g) rindless streaky bacon
- 2 oz (50 g) butter
- 1 onion, finely chopped
- 3 oz (75 g) white breadcrumbs
- 1 oz (25 g) chopped walnuts
- 1 tablespoon chopped fresh parsley
- 1½ lb (675 g) piece topside beef
- 2½ tablespoons plain flour
- 2 teaspoons tomato purée
- 5 fl oz (142 ml) red wine
- 15 fl oz (426 ml) beef stock
- 1 bouquet garni

1 Chop bacon finely. Melt 1 oz (25 g) butter in a pan. Cook bacon and 2 tablespoons chopped onion for 4-5 minutes. Put in a bowl with breadcrumbs, walnuts and parsley. Mix and leave to cool.

2 Cut beef into eight ½ inch (1.3 cm) slices. Beat in a polybag with a rolling pin to ¼ inch (6 mm) thickness.

3 Divide stuffing into eight and spread on slices. Roll up and secure each with string. Melt remaining butter in a 4 pint (2.3 litre) flameproof casserole dish. Cook beef for 3-4 minutes. Add remaining onion, cook for 3-4 minutes. Remove beef. Add flour, cook for 2 minutes. Stir in purée, wine and stock. Bring to boil, stirring, until thickened.

4 Return beef to casserole with bouquet garni. Cover, cook for 1-1½ hours. Remove string.

5 Strain sauce and season well. Skim off fat. Put beef olives on to serving plates and pour over sauce. Serve with herb and garlic tagliatelle, green beans and grilled tomatoes.

TIME: *preparation 25 minutes; cooking 1¾ hours*
NUTRIENTS PER SERVING: *Calories 750; Total fat 59 g; Fibre 2 g; Carbohydrate 21 g*

FOOD EDITOR'S TIP

You can use cocktail sticks to secure the beef olives but do remember to remove them before serving.

Bolognese parcels

- 1 lb (450 g) lean minced beef
- 1 onion, finely sliced
- 1 garlic clove, crushed
- 14 oz (397 g) can tomatoes
- 3 tablespoons tomato purée
- 5 fl oz (142 ml) beef stock
- 4 oz (100 g) button mushrooms, quartered
- 8 spring cabbage leaves

1 Dry-fry mince, onion and garlic for 5 minutes or until mince has browned and onion softened.
2 Add tomatoes, purée and stock. Stir well, bring to boil, then simmer for 30 minutes.
3 Add mushrooms to pan and cook for 15 minutes or until mixture has thickened. Set aside.
4 Meanwhile, remove tough stem from each cabbage leaf. Blanch leaves in boiling water for 1 minute. Drain, pat dry on a clean tea towel.
5 Divide mince mixture evenly between each leaf. Roll up, tucking in ends, and put seam side down into base of an oiled steamer.
6 Steam parcels for 10 minutes or until thoroughly heated. Serve with steamed tomatoes and mashed potatoes with spring onions.

TIME: *preparation 30 minutes; cooking 1 hour*
NUTRIENTS PER SERVING: *Calories 300; Total fat 19 g; Fibre 3 g; Carbohydrate 9 g*

FOOD EDITOR'S TIP

Use young, tender inner cabbage leaves for the best results.

Moroccan beef

- 1 lb (450 g) sirloin steak, trimmed and diced
- ½ teaspoon cayenne pepper
- ½ teaspoon ground cumin
- ½ teaspoon ground coriander
- 2 tablespoons olive oil
- 1 onion, chopped
- 14 oz (397 g) can chopped tomatoes with herbs
- 2 tablespoons tomato purée
- 1 lb (450 g) courgettes, cut into chunks
- 2 oz (50 g) sultanas
- 8 oz (225 g) cracked wheat

1 Put meat in bowl with cayenne pepper, cumin, coriander and 1 tablespoon olive oil. Stir well until lightly coated.
2 Heat remaining oil in saucepan. Add onion, fry for 5 minutes. Add prepared meat, fry for 10 minutes or until browned. Stir in tomatoes and tomato purée, courgettes and sultanas. Simmer, covered, for 40 minutes.
3 Meanwhile, soak cracked wheat in boiling water for 10 minutes or according to packet instructions. Drain and transfer to a saucepan. Cook over a very low heat for 10 minutes. Serve beef with wheat, garnished with chopped mint.

TIME: *preparation 15 minutes; soaking 10 minutes; cooking 55 minutes*
NUTRIENTS PER SERVING: *Calories 500; Total fat 17 g; Fibre 3 g; Carbohydrate 55 g*

FOOD EDITOR'S TIP

If the cracked wheat is a little dry, stir in some melted butter.

Pork stroganoff

- 1 oz (25 g) butter
- 1 tablespoon vegetable oil
- 1¼ lb (550 g) pork tenderloin, cut into ½ inch (1.3 cm) cubes
- 1 onion, finely chopped
- 4 oz (100 g) button mushrooms, sliced
- 6 fl oz (170 ml) single cream

1 Melt butter with oil in a large deep-sided frying pan. Add pork and fry for 5 minutes, stirring frequently. Season well. Stir in the onion and cook for 5 minutes.
2 Stir in mushrooms and cook for 5 minutes. Stir in single cream, and bring to boil. Cook sauce until thickened, sprinkle with parsley and remove from heat.
3 Serve with long grain rice.

TIME: *preparation 5 minutes; cooking 20 minutes*
NUTRIENTS PER SERVING: *Calories 380; Total fat 27 g; Fibre 1 g; Carbohydrate 5 g*

FOOD EDITOR'S TIP

If you are watching calories substitute half of the cream with natural yogurt – it gives the dish a nice tang.

Gingered stir-fry and noodles

- 3 tablespoons dark soy sauce
- 1 tablespoon ground ginger
- 1 tablespoon clear honey
- 1 tablespoon dry sherry
- 1 lb (450 g) pork tenderloin, cut into thin strips
- 2 tablespoons vegetable oil
- 1 inch (2.5 cm) piece root ginger, peeled and sliced into thin strips
- 12 oz (325 g) packet frozen stir-fry vegetables
- 9 oz (250 g) packet thread egg noodles

1 Mix together dark soy sauce, ginger, honey and sherry. Stir in the pork and leave to marinate for 1 hour.
2 Heat oil in a wok or large frying pan. Stir-fry pork with the marinade for 5 minutes. Stir in the ginger and frozen vegetables and cook for 3-4 minutes.
3 Meanwhile, cook noodles in boiling water as directed on packet.
4 Drain noodles and serve with pork mixture, garnished with sliced spring onion.

TIME: *preparation 15 minutes; marinating 1 hour; cooking 9 minutes*
NUTRIENTS PER SERVING: *Calories 500; Total fat 20 g; Fibre 3 g; Carbohydrate 52 g*

FOOD EDITOR'S TIP

This is a perfect main course for a Chinese meal.

Chops with savoury rice

- 10 oz (275 g) basmati rice
- 4 x 4 oz (100 g) boneless pork loin chops
- 2 tablespoons clear honey
- 2 tablespoons soy and garlic sauce
- 2 tablespoons light olive oil
- ¼ teaspoon ground turmeric
- ½ each red, yellow and green pepper, cubed
- 3 spring onions, finely sliced
- 4 oz (100 g) frozen sweetcorn, thawed
- 4 oz (100 g) button mushrooms, quartered

1 Rinse rice in cold water. Put in large saucepan. Add boiling salted water, bring to the boil. Cover and simmer for 10-12 minutes until rice is tender. Drain.
2 Using sharp scissors, trim fat from chops and snip small nicks along rind.
3 Mix together honey and soy and garlic sauce. Brush chops with glaze. Grill for 15 minutes until golden brown, turning once.
4 Meanwhile, heat oil in large frying pan and stir in turmeric, peppers, spring onions, sweetcorn and mushrooms. Cook, stirring occasionally, for 3 minutes.
5 Add rice and seasoning. Cook for further 1 minute or until heated through. Serve rice with chops, garnished with fresh parsley.

TIME: *preparation 15 minutes; cooking 31 minutes*
NUTRIENTS PER SERVING: *Calories 480; Total fat 11 g; Fibre 2 g; Carbohydrate 68 g*

FOOD EDITOR'S TIP

These chops are also great cooked on the barbecue and the rice tastes just as good cold.

Pork cassoulet

- 1 large onion, sliced
- 2 garlic cloves, crushed
- 3 tablespoons olive oil
- 1 lb (450 g) belly pork, trimmed and diced
- 1 lb (450 g) herb pork sausages, halved
- 1 tablespoon paprika
- 14 oz (397 g) can tomatoes
- 2 tablespoons tomato purée
- 4 oz (100 g) canned haricot beans, drained
- 2 thick slices Granary bread, cubed
- 1 oz (25 g) parmesan, grated

1 Fry onion and garlic in 1 tablespoon oil for 5 minutes. Add pork and 1 tablespoon oil, cook for 5 minutes.
2 Remove pork. Add sausages with remaining oil, cook for 10 minutes. Return pork to pan, add paprika, tomatoes, purée and 5 fl oz (142 ml) water. Bring to the boil, stirring occasionally.
3 Add beans to pan. Cover and simmer for 1 hour. Uncover, cook for 15 minutes. Top with bread cubes then parmesan. Grill for 5 minutes.
4 Serve sprinkled with chopped parsley with sautéd leeks and green peppers.

TIME: *preparation 25 minutes; cooking 1 hour 40 minutes*
NUTRIENTS PER SERVING: *Calories 1,080; Total fat 90 g; Fibre 4 g; Carbohydrate 34 g*

FOOD EDITOR'S TIP

Spicy sausages will give the cassoulet extra flavour.

Ham and spinach filo pie

- 8 oz (225 g) frozen chopped spinach
- 4 tablespoons sunflower oil
- 5 oz (125 g) brown cap mushrooms, sliced
- 5 oz (125 g) Greek strained yogurt
- 1 egg (size 3)
- ½ teaspoon ground nutmeg
- 4 sheets frozen filo pastry, thawed
- 1 lb (450 g) cooked ham, chopped
- 2 tablespoons grated parmesan

1 Put spinach in a saucepan and stir over a low heat for about 4 minutes or until thawed. Cover and cook for 2 minutes. Leave to cool.

2 Heat 1 tablespoon oil in a frying pan. Add mushrooms and cook for 1 minute until lightly browned.

3 Mix spinach with the yogurt. Beat in egg, nutmeg and seasoning.

4 Cut four sheets of filo pastry in half. Grease a 9 inch (23 cm) square ovenproof dish with oil. Lay one half sheet of pastry in base and layer up another three half sheets, brushing oil between each.

5 Put ham on top of pastry. Spoon spinach mixture over, then add mushrooms. Season and sprinkle with parmesan.

6 Cover with remaining half sheets of pastry, brushing oil between each. Trim edges, then cut a crisscross pattern on top.

7 Cook pie at 350°F (180°C), Gas 4 for 30 minutes. Increase temperature to 425°F (220°C), Gas 7 for 5-10 minutes until top is crisp and golden. Serve with tomato and spring onion salad and garnish with a sprig of fresh flat leaf parsley.

TIME: *preparation 15 minutes; cooking 46 minutes*
NUTRIENTS PER SERVING: *Calories 430; Total fat 29 g; Fibre 2 g; Carbohydrate 15 g*

FOOD EDITOR'S TIP

The filo pastry makes this a very quick and easy dish to prepare.

Italian pasta salad

- 1 lb (450 g) pipe rigate pasta
- 3 oz (75 g) Italian salami
- 1 oz (25 g) prosciutto
- 1 oz (25 g) bresaola
- 1 oz (25 g) mortadella
- ½ red pepper, cubed
- 1 oz (25 g) pitted black olives
- 1 oz (25 g) pitted green olives
- 2 tablespoons capers
- 1 fl oz (28 ml) light olive oil
- 1 fl oz (28 ml) white wine vinegar
- 1 lemon, juice only
- 1 small bunch basil, torn into pieces

1 Cook pasta in boiling water. Rinse, drain and cool. Put in bowl.

2 Cut salami in half. Thickly shred prosciutto and bresaola. Thinly shred mortadella.

3 Add meats, cubed pepper, black and green olives and capers to pasta. Toss gently.

4 Put olive oil, white wine vinegar, lemon juice, pinch of ground black pepper and basil into screw-top jar. Shake well. Drizzle over salad and toss gently to coat. Serve with crusty bread, if liked.

TIME: *preparation 15 minutes; cooking 10 minutes*
NUTRIENTS PER SERVING: *Calories 650; Total fat 26 g; Fibre 4 g; Carbohydrate 87 g*

FOOD EDITOR'S TIP

Made in larger quantities, this makes a great summer party buffet dish.

Lamb cutlets with rosemary

- 12 x 3 oz (75 g) lamb cutlets
- 2 tablespoons redcurrant jelly
- 5 fl oz (142 ml) port, or lamb stock
- 1 teaspoon red wine vinegar
- 3 sprigs fresh rosemary, or 1 tablespoon dried
- 4 oz (100 g) mushrooms, sliced

1 Season cutlets well. Dry-fry in a large, deep-sided frying pan for 10 minutes, turning once.
2 Mix redcurrant jelly, port or stock, vinegar and rosemary together. Pour into frying pan and boil for 2 minutes or until liquid is reduced by half. Add mushrooms and cook for further 2 minutes. Serve with mixed peas and sweetcorn, cauliflower florets and warm ready-salted crisps, garnished with fresh rosemary.

TIME: *preparation 15 minutes; cooking 14 minutes*
NUTRIENTS PER SERVING: *Calories 290; Total fat 15 g; Fibre Trace; Carbohydrate 5 g*

FOOD EDITOR'S TIP

To warm the crisps put them under a low grill for 5 minutes.

Lamb puffs with potato balls

- ½ oz (15 g) butter
- 1 small onion, finely chopped
- 1 oz (25 g) chestnut mushrooms, finely chopped
- 1 oz (25 g) shiitake mushrooms, finely chopped
- 8 x 3 oz (75 g) lamb cutlets, trimmed
- 1 lb (450 g) fresh puff pastry
- 1 egg (size 3), beaten
- 1½ lb (675 g) potatoes
  vegetable oil for deep frying

1 Melt butter in a pan. Cook onion and mushrooms for 5 minutes. Spoon a little mushroom mixture on to each cutlet. Season well.
2 Thinly roll out pastry to a 14 x 8 inch (35.5 x 20.5 cm) rectangle. Cut into eight 1 inch (2.5 cm) strips. Wrap one strip around each cutlet, covering meat and overlapping slightly. Pinch ends together. Lay cutlets on a wetted baking sheet, spaced apart. Brush with beaten egg.
3 Cook at 400°F (200°C), Gas 6 for 10 minutes. Reduce heat to 375°F (190°C), Gas 5 and cook for a further 20 minutes.
4 Meanwhile, using a melon baller, scoop out potatoes. Heat oil in a pan and deep-fry half of potatoes for 8 minutes or until golden. Drain on kitchen paper. Keep warm. Repeat.
5 Serve with cranberry sauce, aubergines with pine nuts and green beans.

TIME: *preparation 30 minutes; cooking 35 minutes*
NUTRIENTS PER SERVING: *Calories 850; Total fat 48 g; Fibre 3 g; Carbohydrate 78 g*

FOOD EDITOR'S TIP

Take care not to stretch the pastry when wrapping around the cutlets or the filling will leak out.

Spring lamb chops

- 8 x 3 oz (75 g) loin lamb chops
- 3 tablespoons redcurrant jelly
- 1 garlic clove, crushed
- 4 tablespoons orange juice
- 1 tablespoon fresh rosemary
- 10 fl oz (284 ml) lamb stock

1 Using a sharp knife, carefully trim away excess fat from lamb chops and put chops in a shallow glass dish. In a small saucepan, mix together redcurrant jelly, crushed garlic, orange juice and rosemary. Stir over a low heat until redcurrant jelly melts. Remove from heat and leave to cool for 5 minutes.

2 Pour redcurrant and orange mixture over lamb chops and leave to marinate for 30 minutes. Drain chops, reserving marinade.

3 Grill chops under a medium heat for 5 minutes. Turn and cook for a further 5 minutes.

4 Meanwhile, return reserved marinade to small saucepan, bring to boil and simmer for 10 minutes or until mixture is reduced to about 2 tablespoons and is thick and syrupy. Stir in lamb stock and return to boil. Stir well and season to taste.

5 Remove lamb chops from grill and put on warmed serving plates. Garnish with sesame seeds and sprigs of fresh rosemary and serve with redcurrant and orange gravy, boiled new potatoes, steamed baby carrots and spring cabbage.

TIME: *preparation 15 minutes; marinating 30 minutes; cooling 5 minutes; cooking 20 minutes*
NUTRIENTS PER SERVING: *Calories 200; Total fat 9 g; Fibre 0 g; Carbohydrate 9 g*

FOOD EDITOR'S TIP

For the best results, leave the lamb chops to marinate in the redcurrant and orange mixture at room temperature.

Rhogan lamb

- 2 lb (900 g) diced braising lamb
- 2 tablespoons sunflower oil
- 1 large onion, sliced
- 14 oz (400 g) can rhogan curry sauce
- 1 lb (450 g) potatoes
- 1 lb (450 g) cauliflower florets
- 3 oz (75 g) green beans
- 1 red pepper, deseeded and chopped
- 2 tablespoons hot curry paste

1 Trim lamb and fry in oil for 10 minutes until browned. Add onion and fry for 5 minutes.

2 Pour over rhogan sauce and bring to boil. Cover, simmer for 40 minutes until lamb is tender.

3 Meanwhile, cut potatoes into even-sized pieces. Steam for 10 minutes. Add cauliflower florets and beans and steam for 5 minutes. Add chopped pepper and steam for a further 5 minutes or until all vegetables are tender.

4 Mix together hot curry paste with 3 tablespoons water. Heat in a frying pan. Add vegetables and toss together to coat evenly.

5 Serve lamb and vegetables with cucumber raita, and garnished with fresh coriander.

TIME: *preparation 25 minutes; cooking 55 minutes*
NUTRIENTS PER SERVING: *Calories 570; Total fat 31 g; Fibre 5 g; Carbohydrate 29 g*

FOOD EDITOR'S TIP

If preferred, a mild curry paste works equally well.

Brochettes of lamb and pasta

- 4 x 6 oz (150 g) lamb steaks
- 1 orange, juice and rind
- 1 tablespoon paprika
- 4 oz (100 g) button mushrooms
- 3 tablespoons olive oil
- 12 oz (350 g) fresh tagliatelle verdi
- 2 oz (50 g) sun-dried tomatoes, chopped

1 Soak eight wooden skewers in hot water for 10 minutes. Meanwhile, cut lamb into thin strips. Put meat in bowl with orange juice and paprika and marinate for 10 minutes. Thread on to skewers.

2 Put orange rind, mushrooms and oil into a food processor and process for 1 minute. Transfer to a saucepan and cook for 5 minutes. Keep warm over a low heat.

3 Grill lamb for 15 minutes, turning occasionally. Cook pasta in salted boiling water for 3-4 minutes. Drain and toss with mushroom sauce and sun-dried tomatoes. Serve with tomato salad and grated parmesan.

TIME: *preparation 15 minutes; marinating 10 minutes; cooking 19 minutes*

NUTRIENTS PER SERVING: *Calories 480; Total fat 36 g; Fibre 4 g; Carbohydrate 7 g*

FOOD EDITOR'S TIP

The cooking time needs to be adjusted if using dried pasta – check the packet instructions.

Mediterranean soup

- 8 oz (225 g) spaghetti, broken in half
- 2 tablespoons vegetable oil
- 1 medium onion, roughly chopped
- 2 x 14 oz (397 g) cans chopped tomatoes with herbs
- 10 fl oz (284 ml) passata
- 3 x 3½ oz (92 g) frozen cod portions, thawed and cubed
- 6 oz (150 g) frozen, peeled prawns, thawed
- 3½ oz (80 g) can smoked mussels
- 5 fl oz (142 ml) fish stock
- 2 tablespoons fresh mixed herbs, or 2 teaspoons dried

1 Cook spaghetti in boiling water with 1 tablespoon oil for 8 minutes.

2 Meanwhile, heat remaining oil in a saucepan and cook onion for 3 minutes. Drain spaghetti and add to onion with chopped tomatoes.

3 Stir in remaining ingredients, simmer for 6 minutes. Season. Garnish with whole prawns and sprigs of flat leaf parsley. Sprinkle with parmesan before serving, if liked.

TIME: *preparation 5 minutes; cooking 14 minutes*

NUTRIENTS PER SERVING: *Calories 440; Total fat 9 g; Fibre 5 g; Carbohydrate 57 g*

FOOD EDITOR'S TIP

For a really 'smoked' flavour cook the onions in the oil from the canned smoked mussels.

Smoked mackerel pasta

- 2 x 5 oz (125 g) packets Venetian pasta shells
- 2 tablespoons vegetable oil
- 1 medium onion, finely chopped
- 2 tablespoons tomato purée
- 10 fl oz (284 ml) single cream
- 1 teaspoon dried basil
- 4 x 4 oz (100 g) smoked, peppered mackerel fillets, flaked

1 Cook pasta in salted boiling water with 1 tablespoon of the oil for 15 minutes until tender.

2 Meanwhile, heat remaining oil in a large frying pan and cook onion until softened. Stir in tomato purée, cream, basil and smoked mackerel. Season to taste. Cook for 2 minutes.

3 Drain pasta and add to fish mixture. Toss gently to combine. Garnish with fresh basil leaves before serving.

TIME: *preparation 5 minutes; cooking 15 minutes*
NUTRIENTS PER SERVING: *Calories 650; Total fat 38 g; Fibre 2 g; Carbohydrate 50 g*

FOOD EDITOR'S TIP

Be sure to remove the fine bones from the mackerel when flaking it.

Marinated fish kebabs

- 4 tablespoons light olive oil
- 1 lemon
- 1 teaspoon fennel seeds
- 3 tablespoons chopped fresh parsley
- 1lb 2 oz (500 g) packet frozen cod portions, thawed
- 8 king prawns
- 8 red cherry tomatoes
- 8 yellow cherry tomatoes
- 8 fresh bay leaves
- 1 green pepper, cubed

1 Mix together olive oil, lemon juice, fennel seeds, parsley and black pepper. Cut cod portions into large chunks. Put in large bowl with prawns. Pour marinade over and set aside.

2 Thread cod, king prawns, tomatoes, bay leaves and pepper alternately on to eight bamboo skewers. Cook under preheated grill for 12 minutes, turning frequently and brushing with marinade.

3 Serve on a bed of mixed basmati and wild rice, garnished with lemon zest, lemon wedges and fresh chives.

TIME: *preparation 15 minutes; cooking 12 minutes*
NUTRIENTS PER SERVING: *Calories 300; Total fat 15 g; Fibre 2 g; Carbohydrate 5 g*

FOOD EDITOR'S TIP

As an alternative, try substituting whole mushrooms for the prawns.

Seafood savoury rice

- 2 tablespoons olive oil
- 1 onion, finely sliced
- 1 small fennel bulb, finely sliced
- 1 garlic clove, crushed
- 1 small red pepper, deseeded and diced
- 8 oz (225 g) risotto rice
- 1 pint (568 ml) vegetable stock
- 9 oz (250 g) carton prepared mixed seafood, (prawns, mussels, cockles, squid, etc.)
- 2 x 6 oz (150 g) packets small chorizo sausages, sliced
- 2 oz (50 g) frozen petit pois

1 Heat oil in frying pan. Fry onion, fennel, garlic and pepper for 5 minutes until soft.
2 Add rice, cook over a medium heat for 5 minutes or until rice has absorbed oil and is shiny. Stir in 5 fl oz (142 ml) vegetable stock.
3 Stir over a low heat until stock has been absorbed. Stir in seafood, sausages, peas and remaining stock. Bring to boil, stirring.
4 Cover pan, cook over a low heat for 20 minutes until rice is tender. Garnish with fennel fronds, lemon and lime wedges, serve with salad.

TIME: *preparation 15 minutes; cooking 30 minutes*
NUTRIENTS PER SERVING: *Calories 710; Total fat 43 g; Fibre 2 g; Carbohydrate 53 g*

FOOD EDITOR'S TIP

If you can't get a seafood mix use 9 oz (250 g) defrosted cooked prawns for an equally delicious dish.

Piperade gougère

- 1 each red and green pepper, thinly sliced
- 2 oz (50 g) celery, chopped
- 14 oz (397 g) can chopped tomatoes
- 5 fl oz (142 ml) dry white wine
- ½ teaspoon dried oregano
- 2 tablespoons tomato purée
- 4 oz (100 g) butter
- 5 oz (125 g) plain flour, sifted
- 4 eggs (size 3), beaten
- 2 oz (50 g) mature cheddar, grated
- 1 lb (450 g) hoki fillet, skinned and cubed

1 Dry-fry peppers and celery in a nonstick pan for 3 minutes. Add tomatoes, wine, oregano and tomato purée. Simmer for 10 minutes. Put aside.
2 Put butter and 10 fl oz (284 ml) water in a pan and bring to boil, remove from heat. Add flour, stir and leave to cool. Gradually beat in eggs.
3 Spoon choux mixture around edges of a greased 3 pint (1.7 litre) shallow ovenproof dish. Sprinkle with cheese. Cook at 400°F (200°C), Gas 6 for 30 minutes until well risen and golden.
4 Stir hoki into sauce. Simmer for 10 minutes. Spoon sauce into centre of pastry. Serve with broccoli. Garnish with lemon slices and parsley.

TIME: *preparation 30 minutes; cooking 53 minutes*
NUTRIENTS PER SERVING: *Calories 620; Total fat 39 g; Fibre 3 g; Carbohydrate 31 g*

FOOD EDITOR'S TIP

For special occasions put choux mixture into a piping bag fitted with a large plain nozzle and pipe around the edge of four greased individual dishes. Cook as above. Spoon in the sauce and serve in the dishes.

Trout and almonds

- 4 x 4 oz (100 g) rainbow trout, cleaned
- 1 small lemon, grated rind and juice
- 2 oz (50 g) butter
- 2 oz (50 g) flaked almonds

1 Rinse fish under cold running water and pat dry with kitchen paper. Season body cavity well and scatter a little grated lemon rind inside each fish.

2 Melt half of butter in a large frying pan. Add flaked almonds and cook over a medium heat for 2-3 minutes until golden. Remove with a slotted spoon and reserve.

3 Cook trout, two at a time, in frying pan with remaining butter for 4 minutes each side or until tender and flesh is opaque. Drain on kitchen paper. Keep hot while cooking remaining trout.

4 Return almonds to pan and add lemon juice. Reheat gently for 1 minute. Garnish fish with lemon twists and fresh dill and serve scattered with almonds, with sautéed scallop potatoes, baby sweetcorn and broccoli.

TIME: *preparation 10 minutes; cooking 20 minutes.*
NUTRIENTS PER SERVING: *Calories 300; Total fat 21 g; Fibre 1 g; Carbohydrate 0 g*

FOOD EDITOR'S TIP

If you prefer, ask your fishmonger to fillet the fish first. Cook fillets for 3 minutes each side until tender. Serve as above.

Salmon parcels with vegetables

- 4 x 4 oz (100 g) salmon fillets, skinned
- 8 sheets fresh filo pastry
- 1½ oz (40 g) butter, melted
- 150 g packet full-fat soft cheese with garlic and herbs
- 8 oz (225 g) button mushrooms, wiped
- 2 courgettes, sliced
- 2 tablespoons olive oil
- 1 small lemon, grated rind only

1 Remove any bones from salmon. Brush four sheets of filo pastry with a little melted butter. Put each remaining filo sheet on top of a buttered sheet to create a double layer of pastry. Put one salmon fillet in the centre of each double layer.

2 Divide soft cheese into four equal pieces and spread over top of each salmon fillet. Wrap filo around fish to form a parcel, tuck ends under and put seam side down on a greased baking sheet.

3 Brush with remaining butter and cook at 375°F (190°C), Gas 5 for 30 minutes, until pastry is golden and salmon tender.

4 Meanwhile, fry mushrooms and courgettes together in olive oil for 5 minutes. Add lemon rind and cook for 3 minutes until vegetables are tender and golden.

5 Serve salmon parcels, lemony mushrooms and courgettes with steamed new potatoes and green beans, garnished with a twist of lemon and fresh dill.

TIME: *preparation 25 minutes; cooking 30 minutes*
NUTRIENTS PER SERVING: *Calories 580; Total fat 40 g; Fibre 1 g; Carbohydrate 29 g*

FOOD EDITOR'S TIP

If the filo parcels start to over-brown cover with foil.

Citrus mackerel and rice

- 4 x 6 oz (150 g) mackerel, cleaned
- 1 lemon, sliced and halved
- ½ cucumber, chopped
- 1 teaspoon sugar
- 1 tablespoon white wine vinegar
- ½ each red and yellow pepper, deseeded and diced
- 1 small fennel bulb, trimmed and sliced
- 4 spring onions, trimmed and sliced
- 2 tablespoons olive oil
- 8 oz (225 g) easy-cook long grain rice
- 15 fl oz (426 ml) fish stock

1 Remove fish heads and discard. Cut three slits in each fish. Put lemon slices into slits, season.
2 In a bowl mix together cucumber, sugar and vinegar. Cover, chill until required.
3 Cook peppers, fennel and spring onions in 1 tablespoon olive oil for 2-3 minutes. Add rice and cook, stirring occasionally, for 5 minutes.
4 Add stock, bring to the boil. Simmer uncovered for 10 minutes until stock is absorbed.
5 Meanwhile, brush fish with remaining oil, grill 3-4 minutes each side. Garnish with fennel.

TIME: *preparation 20 minutes; cooking 18 minutes*
NUTRIENTS PER SERVING: *Calories 680; Total fat 37 g; Fibre 2 g; Carbohydrate 49 g*

FOOD EDITOR'S TIP

Be careful when seasoning rice as fish stock can be quite salty.

Salmon fillet with tarragon

- 2 large baking potatoes
- 6 oz (150 g) butter
- 1 tablespoon olive oil
- 4 x 6 oz (150 g) fresh salmon fillets
- 3 oz (75 g) cheddar, grated
- 1 tablespoon mixed peppercorns in brine
- 2 teaspoons wine vinegar
- 2 tablespoons chopped fresh tarragon

1 Put potatoes on to a baking sheet and cook at 350°F (180°C), Gas 4 for 1 hour until tender.
2 Take potatoes out of oven, cut in half and scoop out flesh. Put into a bowl and mix with 2 oz (50 g) butter and grated cheese. Refill potato halves and grill for 3 minutes.
3 Melt 2 oz (50 g) butter with oil in a large frying pan. Add salmon fillets flesh side down and cook gently for 4-5 minutes. Turn over and cook for a further 4-5 minutes. Keep warm.
4 Add peppercorns and wine vinegar and remaining butter to pan and heat for 1 minute. Stir in tarragon and pour over salmon. Serve with potatoes, courgettes and salad. Garnish with lemon.

TIME: *preparation 15 minutes; cooking 1 hour 14 minutes*
NUTRIENTS PER SERVING: *Calories 750; Total fat 58 g; Fibre 2 g; Carbohydrate 22 g*

FOOD EDITOR'S TIP

Peppercorns are quite hot so you can substitute with flaked almonds if you prefer.

VEGETARIAN

Crispy stuffed marrow

- 2 oz (50 g) red lentils
- 2 oz (50 g) green lentils
- 1 pint (568 ml) vegetable stock
- 2 onions, finely chopped
- 1 garlic clove, crushed
- 1 tablespoon sunflower oil
- 4 oz (100 g) button mushrooms, sliced
- 2 tablespoons tomato purée
- 2 lb (900 g) marrow, halved lengthways
- 1 oz (25 g) wholemeal breadcrumbs
- 1½ oz (40 g) vegetarian cheddar, grated

1   Put lentils in a pan with 1 pint (568 ml) boiling water, soak for 30 minutes. Drain, return to pan and add stock. Simmer for 30 minutes. Drain.
2   Fry onions and garlic in oil until golden. Add lentils, mushrooms and tomato purée. Cook for 2 minutes. Season well.
3   Deseed marrow halves. Put on a baking sheet, spoon lentil mixture down centre.
4   Sprinkle with breadcrumbs and cheese. Cook at 350°F (180°C), Gas 4 for 30 minutes. Serve with tomatoes and buttered tagliatelle garnished with orange rind and flat leaf parsley.

TIME: *preparation 20 minutes; soaking 30 minutes; cooking 1 hour*
NUTRIENTS PER SERVING: *Calories 225; Total fat 13 g; Fibre 9 g; Carbohydrate 30 g*

FOOD EDITOR'S TIP

The lentil filling freezes well so you could prepare this in advance.

Country mushrooms

- 3 oz (75 g) couscous
- 10 fl oz (284 ml) hot vegetable stock
- 4 thick slices white bread
- 5 tablespoons olive oil
- ½ bunch spring onions, sliced
- ½ small red chilli, sliced
- 2 garlic cloves, crushed
- 12 medium-sized flat mushrooms
- 2 oz (50 g) vegetarian cheddar, grated

1 Soak couscous in stock for 5 minutes or until soft. Drain off excess stock. Meanwhile, using 3 tablespoons oil, fry bread in two batches, for 3 minutes each batch, until golden. Drain, keep hot.
2 Fry spring onions, chilli and garlic for 5 minutes until tender. Drain, stir into couscous. Season.
3 Meanwhile, brush mushrooms with 2 tablespoons olive oil and cook under preheated grill for 5 minutes until tender, turning once.
4 Arrange mushrooms on bread and spoon couscous mixture on top. Sprinkle over cheddar and grill for 2 minutes. Garnish with chopped parsley and serve with winter salad and toasted flaked almonds.

TIME: *preparation 20 minutes; cooking 13 minutes*
NUTRIENTS PER SERVING: *Calories 370; Total fat 22 g; Fibre 4 g; Carbohydrate 34 g*

FOOD EDITOR'S TIP

You don't need to peel the mushrooms, simply wipe them with damp kitchen paper.

Nutty gnocchi

- 1lb (450 g) ricotta, sieved
- 4 oz (100 g) butter, melted
- 2 oz (50 g) parmesan, grated
- 1 egg (size 3), beaten
- 6 oz (150 g) plain wholemeal flour
- pinch of ground nutmeg
- 2 oz (50 g) pine nuts
- 1 oz (25 g) walnuts, finely chopped
- 4 tablespoons pesto sauce
- 15¾ oz (440 g) jar tomato pasta sauce

1 Beat together ricotta, butter, parmesan, egg, flour and nutmeg until smooth. Divide ricotta gnocchi into 36 equal pieces.
2 On a well-floured surface, pat each piece into a 3 inch (7.5 cm) circle. Mix together nuts and pesto sauce. Spoon ½ teaspoon pesto filling into centres, fold in half, pinching edges together. Trim edges and mark with a fork.
3 Steam a third of gnocchi for 6 minutes or until firm. Keep hot. Repeat with remaining gnocchi. Heat tomato pasta sauce in a pan.
4 Serve gnocchi with sauce. Sprinkle over parmesan, garnish with lemon wedges and fresh basil. Serve with bread and salad leaves.

TIME: *preparation 40 minutes; cooking 18 minutes*
NUTRIENTS PER SERVING: *Calories 800; Total fat 62 g; Fibre 10 g; Carbohydrate 35 g*

FOOD EDITOR'S TIP

If you don't have a steamer place a wire rack over a frying pan of simmering water. Put gnocchi on rack and cover with foil.

Vegetable quiche

- 6 oz (150 g) plain flour
- 3 oz (75 g) block margarine
- 1 onion, thinly sliced
- 4 oz (100 g) frozen, diced mixed peppers, thawed and drained
- 3 oz (75 g) baby sweetcorn, halved
- 8 oz (225 g) frozen broccoli florets, thawed
- 2 eggs (size 3)
- 10 fl oz (284 ml) milk
- 2 oz (50 g) vegetarian cheddar, grated

1. Sift flour into a bowl and rub in margarine. Stir in enough water to form a soft dough.
2. Roll out to line a 9½ inch (24 cm) fluted, loose-bottomed flan tin. Prick base, chill for 30 minutes.
3. Meanwhile, dry-fry onion for 2-3 minutes. Add remaining vegetables, cook for 5 minutes. Drain.
4. Bake pastry case blind at 400°F (200°C), Gas 6 for 10 minutes. Remove lining and cook for 10 minutes. Reduce oven to 375°F (190°C), Gas 5.
5. Spoon vegetables into pastry case. Beat eggs with milk. Season, pour over, sprinkle with cheddar. Cook for 40 minutes. Serve with chips and salad.

TIME: *preparation 35 minutes; chilling 30 minutes; cooking 1 hour 8 minutes*
NUTRIENTS PER SERVING: *Calories 440; Total fat 25 g; Fibre 4 g; Carbohydrate 38 g*

FOOD EDITOR'S TIP

Take care not to over-season the quiche as the cheese can be rather salty.

Mushroom melts

- 12 large flat mushrooms
- 3 oz (75 g) basmati rice
- 15¼ oz (432 g) canned red kidney beans, rinsed and drained
- 1 red pepper, deseeded and finely chopped
- 6 oz (150 g) mozzarella, cubed
- 2 oz (50 g) gruyère, cubed
- 2 tablespoons chopped fresh parsley
- 2 oz (50 g) parmesan

1. Wash rice and put in saucepan with a little salt. Cover with cold water and bring to boil. Reduce heat, stir and cook for 20 minutes.
2. Pull out stalks from mushrooms, wipe and finely chop. Put chopped mushroom stalks into a bowl and stir in cooked rice, red kidney beans, chopped pepper, mozzarella, gruyère and chopped parsley. Mix together gently.
3. Divide rice and vegetable filling evenly between mushroom caps. Sprinkle parmesan over each filled mushroom. Cook under a preheated grill for 10 minutes until bubbling.
4. Garnish with lemon wedges and serve with brown bread.

TIME: *preparation 20 minutes; cooking 30 minutes*
NUTRIENTS PER SERVING: *Calories 490; Total fat 18 g; Fibre 8 g; Carbohydrate 53 g*

FOOD EDITOR'S TIP

If the mushrooms are quite thick, fry for 1-2 minutes before filling and grilling.

Potato pan-fry

- 7 tablespoons sunflower oil
- 1 onion, thinly sliced
- 1 each red and green pepper, deseeded and diced
- 4 baking potatoes, sliced and parboiled
- 6 eggs (size 3)
- 5 fl oz (142 ml) single cream
- 15¼ oz (432 g) can kidney beans, drained
- 15¼ oz (432 g) can borlotti beans, drained
- 15¼ oz (432 g) can chickpeas, drained
- 2 sticks celery, chopped
- 2 tablespoons chopped fresh parsley
- 3 teaspoons white wine vinegar
- 2 oz (50 g) vegetarian cheddar, grated

1   Heat 4 tablespoons oil in a large frying pan. Stir-fry onion and peppers for 5 minutes. Remove.
2   Layer potatoes, onion and peppers alternately in frying pan. Whisk together eggs and single cream. Season. Pour over vegetables. Cover and cook for 10 minutes or until set.
3   Mix together beans, chickpeas, celery, parsley, vinegar and remaining oil. Season. Uncover pan, sprinkle over cheddar. Grill for 2-3 minutes. Serve with bean and mixed leaf salads.

TIME: *preparation 25 minutes; cooking 18 minutes*
NUTRIENTS PER SERVING: *Calories 840; Total fat 34 g; Fibre 24 g; Carbohydrate 101 g*

FOOD EDITOR'S TIP

Parboil potato slices for about 8 minutes or until just tender. Be careful not to overcook or they will break up.

Saucy pasta and hot bread

- 2 x 9 oz (250 g) packets fresh tortellini
- pinch of salt
- 2 x 14 oz (397 g) cans chopped tomatoes with herbs
- 3 tablespoons tomato purée
- 2 teaspoons caster sugar
- 2 garlic cloves, crushed
- 2 tablespoons pesto sauce
- 3 tablespoons olive oil
- 1 ciabatta loaf

1   Add pasta and a pinch of salt to a pan of boiling water. Return to boil. Simmer for 12 minutes or as directed on packet. Drain.
2   Meanwhile, put tomatoes into a large pan with tomato purée, sugar and garlic. Simmer gently for 8 minutes until thickened.
3   Mix together pesto and olive oil. Slice bread and spread with pesto mixture. Grill for 2 minutes, turning, until golden.
4   Divide pasta between serving plates. Pour over tomato sauce. Garnish with grated fresh parmesan and chopped fresh parsley. Serve with grilled pesto ciabatta bread.

TIME: *preparation 15 minutes; cooking 12 minutes*
NUTRIENTS PER SERVING: *Calories 870; Total fat 20 g; Fibre 13 g; Carbohydrate 156 g*

FOOD EDITOR'S TIP

Ready-made tortellini has a variety of fillings, so ring the changes.

Potato pizza slice

- 10.2 oz (290 g) packet pizza base mix
- 3 tablespoons tomato purée
- 10½ oz (290 g) jar condiverdi with peppers and sun-dried tomatoes
- 1 tablespoon chopped fresh rosemary, or ½ tablespoon dried
- 2 medium onions, finely sliced
- 8 oz (225 g) potatoes, very finely sliced
- 4 tablespoons olive oil
- 2 each red and yellow peppers, deseeded and cut into quarters

1 Make up packet pizza base mix with 4 fl oz (114 ml) hand-hot water, according to packet instructions. Knead dough on a lightly floured surface for 5 minutes, until smooth and elastic.
2 Roll out dough and use to line base and sides of an 11 x 7 inch (28 x 18 cm) oiled Swiss roll tin.
3 Spread tomato purée and condiverdi over pizza base to within 1/2 inch (1.3 cm) of edges. Sprinkle with rosemary. Arrange onion slices and potatoes on top, overlapping each slightly. Drizzle over 3 tablespoons olive oil. Cook at 425°F (220°C), Gas 7 for 30 minutes.
4 Brush pepper quarters with remaining olive oil and grill for last 10 minutes of pizza cooking time. Serve with pizza and steamed spinach. Garnish with fresh basil.

TIME: *preparation 15 minutes; cooking 30 minutes*
NUTRIENTS PER SERVING: *Calories 450; Total fat 15 g; Fibre 6 g; Carbohydrate 70 g*

FOOD EDITOR'S TIP

Condiverdi are a range of Italian ingredients preserved in oil. Look for them in jars in the condiment section of the supermarket.

Summer pasta salad

- 12 oz (325 g) three-colour pasta spirals
- 4 oz (100 g) baby carrots, trimmed
- 4 oz (100 g) baby sweetcorn, halved lengthways
- 2 oz (50 g) mangetout, shredded
- 4 oz (100 g) asparagus sprue, trimmed
- 4 spring onions, trimmed and sliced
- 1 tablespoon pesto sauce
- 1 garlic clove, crushed
- 1 teaspoon lemon juice
- 4 tablespoons virgin olive oil
- 3 tablespoons chopped fresh flat leaf parsley
- 12 black olives

1 Cook the pasta in a large pan of lightly salted boiling water for 8-10 minutes or according to packet instructions.
2 Meanwhile, blanch the carrots and sweetcorn for 2 minutes. Add the mangetout and asparagus and cook for a further 3 minutes or until all are just tender. Drain well.
3 Put the pesto sauce, garlic, lemon juice, oil and seasoning into a screw-top jar. Shake well to combine.
4 Drain pasta and toss in pesto dressing while still warm. Add vegetables, parsley and olives, toss gently and serve.

TIME: *preparation 20 minutes; cooking 10 minutes*
NUTRIENTS PER SERVING: *Calories 210; Total fat 19 g; Fibre 4 g; Carbohydrate 7 g*

FOOD EDITOR'S TIP

If the carrots are much bigger than the sweetcorn split them in half.

Vegetable pasta gratin

- 1 small aubergine, thinly sliced
- 1 oz (25 g) salt
- 1 lb (450 g) pipe regate pasta
- 8 oz (225 g) courgettes, sliced diagonally
- 8 oz (225 g) leeks, sliced thinly
- 1 oz (25 g) butter
- 1 oz (25 g) plain flour
- 1 pint (568 ml) skimmed milk
- 2 oz (50 g) white breadcrumbs
- 2 oz (50 g) vegetarian cheddar, grated

1   Sprinkle aubergine slices with salt and leave for
    30 minutes. Rinse in cold water, pat dry and steam with
    courgettes and leeks for 5 minutes until tender.
2   Meanwhile, cook pasta in salted boiling water. Rinse, drain
    and cool. Melt butter in large pan, add flour and stir over
    low heat for 1 minute. Remove from heat and gradually
    add milk. Stir over medium heat until sauce boils and is
    smooth and thick. Season well.
3   Stir pasta into sauce and cook gently for further 2 minutes,
    stirring continuously.
4   Grease a shallow 3 pint (1.7 litre) dish. Put half pasta
    mixture into serving dish, cover with steamed vegetables
    and top with remaining pasta.
5   Mix together breadcrumbs and grated cheddar. Sprinkle
    evenly over pasta. Cook for 3 minutes under preheated grill
    until golden brown. Serve with salad leaves and cherry
    tomatoes.

TIME: *preparation 15 minutes; standing 30 minutes; cooking 15 minutes*
NUTRIENTS PER SERVING: *Calories 400; Total fat 12 g; Fibre 5 g; Carbohydrate 59 g*

FOOD EDITOR'S TIP

You can also make this for non-vegetarians, adding 8 oz (225 g) diced
cooked ham to the pasta sauce and using a mature cheddar.

Cauliflower omelette

- 1 lb (450 g) cauliflower florets
- 10 fl oz (284 ml) milk
- 1 tablespoon cornflour
- 3 oz (75 g) vegetarian cheddar, grated
- 1 tablespoon dried parsley
- 4 tablespoons vegetable oil
- 8 eggs (size 3), beaten

1   Cook cauliflower florets in boiling water for 5 minutes or
    until just tender. Drain.
2   Mix 4 tablespoons milk and the cornflour to a smooth
    paste. Heat remaining milk and stir in. Cook over a low
    heat until thickened. Stir in cheese and parsley. Remove
    from heat.
3   Heat 1 tablespoon oil in an omelette or frying pan. Pour in
    one-quarter of the beaten eggs. Season, cook over a
    medium heat for 3-4 minutes.
4   Spoon over one-quarter of the cauliflower florets and fold
    the omelette in half. Keep hot.
5   Make three more omelettes. Reheat sauce for 1 minute and
    drizzle over each. Serve with steamed beans and carrots,
    and garnish with watercress.

TIME: *preparation 15 minutes; cooking 22 minutes*
NUTRIENTS PER SERVING: *Calories 520; Total fat 37 g; Fibre 7 g; Carbohydrate 17 g*

FOOD EDITOR'S TIP

For a quicker version, stir cooked cauliflower florets into eggs, and
cook all together in a large pan. Finish cooking under a preheated
grill. Cut into four and serve with sauce.

Tomato and lentil bolognese

- 2 oz (50 g) red lentils
- 2 oz (50 g) green split peas
- 1¼ pints (994 ml) vegetable stock
- 1 onion, finely chopped
- 1 garlic clove, crushed
- 1 tablespoon vegetable oil
- 14 oz (397 g) can chopped tomatoes
- 6 oz (150 g) mushrooms, sliced
- 3 tablespoons tomato purée
- pinch of mixed herbs
- pinch of sugar
- 10 oz (275 g) wholewheat spaghetti
- 1 tablespoon chopped fresh parsley

1 Spread out lentils and peas on a flat plate. Discard any discoloured ones.
2 Put into large saucepan and cover with boiling water. Return to the boil. Turn off heat, cover with lid and leave to soak for 30 minutes.
3 Drain, return pulses to pan and, stirring continuously, add 1 pint (568 ml) vegetable stock. Simmer for 30 minutes or until pulses are tender.
4 Fry onion and garlic in oil until golden brown. Add to pulses and cook for 2 minutes.
5 Stir in tomatoes, mushrooms, tomato purée, herbs, sugar and seasoning with remaining stock. Return to boil then simmer for 15 minutes.
6 Meanwhile, put spaghetti in large saucepan with boiling water. Return to boil and cook for 10 minutes until tender. Drain, add chopped fresh parsley and toss together well.
7 Spoon on to serving plates and top with bolognese sauce. Serve with grated parmesan.

TIME: *preparation 15 minutes; soaking 30 minutes; cooking 47 minutes*
NUTRIENTS PER SERVING: *Calories 375; Total fat 6 g; Fibre 10 g; Carbohydrate 67 g*

FOOD EDITOR'S TIP

Use dried mixed herbs sparingly as they are very pungent.

Spinach bake

- 1 lb (450 g) frozen chopped spinach, thawed
- 2 lb (900 g) potatoes, parboiled
- 1 lb (450 g) tomatoes, thinly sliced
- 4 oz (100 g) vegetarian cheddar, grated
- 1 onion, finely chopped
- 1 lb (450 g) jar tomato and herb sauce
- 1 teaspoon chopped parsley

1 Put spinach into a large sieve and press firmly with back of a wooden spoon to squeeze out excess liquid.
2 Cut potatoes into ¼ inch (6 mm) slices. Layer tomatoes, cheese, spinach and potato slices alternately in a greased 2½ pint (1.4 litre) soufflé dish, finishing with a layer of potato.
3 Cook at 375°F (190°C), Gas 5 for 45 minutes until top is golden and bubbling. Set aside.
4 Meanwhile, dry-fry onion in a nonstick pan for 3 minutes. Stir in tomato sauce and parsley. Cover and simmer for 5 minutes.
5 Turn bake on to a serving plate and cut into thick wedges. Serve with tomato sauce, sweetcorn, sautéed mushrooms and salad.

TIME: *preparation 25 minutes; cooking 45 minutes*
NUTRIENTS PER SERVING: *Calories 380; Total fat 15 g; Fibre 7 g; Carbohydrate 49 g*

FOOD EDITOR'S TIP

If you've got a food processor try using it to slice the potatoes.

Veggie burgers with chunky chips

- 2 oz (50 g) dried mixed beans, soaked overnight
- 1 small onion, finely chopped
- 1 carrot, grated
- 1 teaspoon vegetable extract
- 1 teaspoon dried mixed herbs
- 1 oz (25 g) wholemeal breadcrumbs
- 4 medium baking potatoes
- 5 fl oz (142 ml) vegetable oil
- 4 sesame seed baps

1 Drain soaked beans and rinse. Put in large saucepan and cover with cold water. Bring to boil. Boil for 10 minutes then reduce heat and simmer for 1 hour until beans are soft. Drain well.
2 Put beans into food processor with chopped onion, grated carrot, vegetable extract, mixed herbs and wholemeal breadcrumbs. Mix together well until almost smooth. Stir in seasoning.
3 Using wetted hands, shape mixture into four burgers. Chill.
4 Cut baking potatoes into chunky chips. Heat oil in a shallow frying pan and fry chips in two batches until tender and golden. Drain on kitchen paper before serving.
5 Meanwhile, split baps and toast under a hot grill. Brush burgers with oil and grill for 15 minutes, turning once.
6 Serve burgers in baps with chips, tomatoes, salad and sweetcorn relish.

TIME: *Soaking overnight; preparation 20 minutes; cooking 1 hour 25 minutes*
NUTRIENTS PER SERVING: *Calories 410; Total fat 9 g; Fibre 6 g; Carbohydrate 73 g*

FOOD EDITOR'S TIP

The burger mixture can also be used for making vegetarian 'sausage' rolls.

Peanut pilaf

- 2 tablespoons vegetable oil
- 1 medium onion, roughly chopped
- 1 each red and green pepper, finely diced
- 12 oz (325 g) basmati rice
- 12 fl oz (341 ml) hot vegetable stock
- 3 eggs (size 3), beaten
- 1 tablespoon light soy sauce
- 2 oz (50 g) salted peanuts

1 Heat 1 tablespoon oil in large frying pan and cook chopped onion and peppers for 5-6 minutes or until tender.
2 Add rice and hot vegetable stock. Return to boil and simmer for 10 minutes or until rice is tender. Keep hot.
3 Beat eggs together with seasoning. Heat remaining oil in large frying pan, add egg mixture. Spread out thinly. Cook for 2 minutes over low heat until base is set.
4 Flip omelette over using a fish slice and cook for 2 minutes. Turn out on to plate, roll up tightly and cut into thin slices.
5 Stir soy sauce and peanuts into rice mixture. Garnish with omelette slices and serve with extra peanuts.

TIME: *preparation 15 minutes; cooking 18 minutes*
NUTRIENTS PER SERVING: *Calories 520; Total fat 18 g; Fibre 2 g; Carbohydrate 72 g*

FOOD EDITOR'S TIP

Dry roasted peanuts may be added to the rice for a different flavour. To perk up the omelette, add 1 tablespoon chopped fresh chives or fresh coriander at step 3.

Rich cheese pasties

- 1 oz (25 g) butter
- 1 onion, thinly sliced
- 1 oz (25 g) plain flour
- 10 fl oz (284 ml) milk
- pinch of grated nutmeg
- 2 tablespoons chopped fresh parsley
- 4 oz (100 g) cooked rice
- 4 oz (100 g) vegetarian cheddar, grated
- 8 oz (225 g) puff pastry, thawed if frozen
- beaten egg to glaze

1   Melt butter in saucepan. Add onion and fry until golden. Stir in flour. Cook, stirring, for 1 minute. Remove from heat and stir in milk.
2   Stir sauce over a low heat until thickened. Stir in nutmeg, parsley and seasoning with rice and two-thirds of the cheddar.
3   Roll out pastry to a 14 inch (36 cm) square. Cut into four 7 inch (18 cm) squares. Spoon filling into centre of each square.
4   Dampen pastry edges, fold in half and seal. Flute edges and brush with beaten egg. Sprinkle with remaining grated cheddar.
5   Put pasties on a greased baking sheet, spaced a little apart, and cook at 400°F (200°C), Gas 6 for 20 minutes or until golden. Serve with avocado and mixed salad.

TIME: *preparation 20 minutes; cooking 22 minutes*
NUTRIENTS PER SERVING: *Calories 450; Total fat 29 g; Fibre 1 g; Carbohydrate 37 g*

FOOD EDITOR'S TIP

To save time you could use canned cooked rice.

Spicy vegetable curry

- 4 oz (100 g) dried mixed beans, soaked overnight
- 2 tablespoons vegetable oil
- 1 large onion, chopped
- 1 garlic clove, crushed
- 1 oz (25 g) fresh root ginger, grated
- 1 tablespoon plain flour
- 1 tablespoon tomato purée
- 1 pint (568 ml) hot vegetable stock
- 1 each red and green pepper, chopped
- 1 large courgette, sliced
- 1 aubergine, chopped
- 6 oz (150 g) okra, sliced
- 1 lb (450 g) potatoes, cubed
- 6 oz (150 g) French beans
- 14 oz (397 g) can chopped tomatoes
- 2 large carrots, roughly chopped
- 4 oz (100 g) cooked mixed beans
- 3 oz (75 g) sultanas
- 1 oz (25 g) garam masala

1   Drain soaked beans and rinse. Put in large saucepan and cover with cold water. Bring to boil. Boil for 10 minutes, reduce heat, simmer 1 hour until beans are soft. Drain well.
2   Heat oil and fry onion and garlic in large pan until golden brown. Add grated root ginger and cook for 2 minutes.
3   Meanwhile, mix together flour and tomato purée with enough of the vegetable stock to make a smooth paste, then stir into pan with remaining stock.
4   Add all remaining vegetables, mixed beans and sultanas to frying pan. Bring to the boil and simmer for 45 minutes or until all vegetables are tender.
5   Stir in garam masala. Garnish each plate with some fresh coriander and serve with naan bread and a tomato and onion salad.

TIME: *preparation 15 minutes; cooking 1 hour 55 minutes*
NUTRIENTS PER SERVING: *Calories 600; Total fat 13 g; Fibre 16 g; Carbohydrate 107 g*

FOOD EDITOR'S TIP

If you can't find okra, use more courgettes instead.

Spicy tomatoes

- 1 garlic clove, crushed
- 2 oz (50 g) button mushrooms, sliced
- 2 tablespoons sunflower oil
- 3 oz (75 g) brown basmati rice
- 10 fl oz (284 ml) vegetable stock
- 4 spring onions, sliced
- 4 beef tomatoes
- ½ teaspoon ground coriander
- ¼ teaspoon ground cumin
- 1 oz (25 g) flaked almonds, toasted
- 1 teaspoon chopped fresh coriander

1 Fry garlic and mushrooms in oil for 5 minutes until soft. Add rice and cook, stirring frequently, for 2-3 minutes. Pour in vegetable stock, bring to boil, cover and simmer for 20 minutes. Stir in spring onions 5 minutes before end of cooking time and cook until rice is tender.
2 Meanwhile, cut a lid from top of each tomato and a small slice from each base. Using a teaspoon, remove flesh, leaving about ¼ inch (6 mm) inside each tomato shell. Roughly chop flesh. Reserve 4 tablespoons.
3 Stir remaining tomato flesh, ground coriander, cumin and toasted flaked almonds into rice mixture and season well.
4 Spoon rice mixture into each tomato shell. Stand stuffed tomatoes on a greased baking sheet and cook at 350°F (180°C), Gas 4 for 15 minutes. Remove from oven and sprinkle with chopped coriander. Serve with courgettes and reserved tomato flesh, baby sweetcorn and garlic and herb bread.

TIME: *preparation 15 minutes; cooking 43 minutes*
NUTRIENTS PER SERVING: *Calories 190; Total fat 11 g; Fibre 3 g; Carbohydrate 18 g*

FOOD EDITOR'S TIP

If you find that filling the tomatoes is too fiddly, serve the rice mixture with sliced grilled tomatoes on top.

Cheesy bake

- 10 oz (275 g) frozen chopped spinach
- 1 garlic clove, crushed
- 8 oz (225 g) full-fat soft cheese
- 2 oz (50 g) walnut pieces, finely chopped
- ¼ teaspoon grated nutmeg
- 12 cannelloni tubes
- 10 oz (275 g) natural yogurt
- 1 tablespoon cornflour
- 2 eggs (size 3)
- 1 oz (25 g) vegetarian cheddar, grated
- 1 oz (25 g) parmesan, grated

1 Cook spinach, stirring occasionally, until all water has evaporated. Cool. Beat in garlic, soft cheese, nuts and nutmeg. Season well.
2 Divide mixture into twelve portions and spoon into cannelloni tubes. Put in base of a greased shallow 2½ pint (1.4 litre) ovenproof dish.
3 Beat together yogurt, cornflour, eggs and seasoning. Pour over cannelloni. Sprinkle over cheddar and parmesan. Bake at 375°F (190°C), Gas 5 for 25-35 minutes or until cannelloni is tender and topping is golden. Serve hot with tomato and onion and a mixed leaf salad.

TIME: *preparation 25 minutes; cooking 35 minutes*
NUTRIENTS PER SERVING: *Calories 500; Total fat 33 g; Fibre 2 g; Carbohydrate 33 g*

FOOD EDITOR'S TIP

For a lower fat version, use low-fat cheese and yogurt.

Peanut chop suey

- 9 oz (250 g) packet medium egg noodles
- 2 tablespoons sunflower oil
- 2 x 12½ oz (355 g) packets fresh Chinese stir-fry vegetables
- ½ bunch spring onions, trimmed and sliced
- 4 oz (100 g) salted peanuts
- 2 tablespoons light soy sauce
- 2 tablespoons mushroom ketchup
- 2 eggs (size 2), hard-boiled, shelled and sliced

1 Put noodles into a bowl. Pour over boiling water and leave to soak for 4 minutes or according to instructions on packet.
2 Meanwhile, heat oil in a large frying pan or wok. Stir-fry Chinese vegetables and spring onions for 3-4 minutes. Stir in peanuts, soy sauce and mushroom ketchup. Stir-fry for 2-3 minutes.
3 Drain noodles and add to vegetable mixture. Spoon on to serving plates. Arrange sliced eggs on top. Serve garnished with shredded spring onion.

TIME: *preparation 15 minutes; cooking 7 minutes*
NUTRIENTS PER SERVING: *Calories 550; Total fat 28 g; Fibre 8 g; Carbohydrate 59 g*

FOOD EDITOR'S TIP

You should find mushroom ketchup near the speciality sauces in the supermarket; if it's unavailable use 2 tablespoons dry sherry instead.

Mushroom roulade

- 1 lb (450 g) frozen chopped spinach
- 2 garlic cloves, crushed
- 4 oz (100 g) vegetarian cheddar, grated
- ¼ teaspoon grated nutmeg
- 4 eggs (size 3), separated
- 1 oz (25 g) parmesan, grated
- 2 oz (50 g) button mushrooms, chopped
- 1 oz (25 g) butter, melted
- 1 oz (25 g) plain flour
- 10 fl oz (284 ml) milk
- 1 tablespoon coarse grain mustard

1 Grease and line a 13 x 9 inch (33 x 23 cm) Swiss roll tin with nonstick baking paper. Cook spinach, stirring, until water has evaporated. Stir in garlic, 2 oz (50 g) cheddar and the nutmeg. Cool. Stir in egg yolks.
2 Whisk egg whites until stiff peaks form. Fold into spinach mixture. Pour into tin. Cook at 400°F (200°C), Gas 6 for 8-10 minutes until firm.
3 Sprinkle a sheet of nonstick paper with parmesan. Turn out roulade on to paper. Cool.
4 Fry mushrooms in butter. Add flour, cook for 1 minute. Gradually stir in milk. Stir over a low heat until sauce boils and thickens. Stir in mustard, remaining cheddar and seasoning.
5 Remove paper from roulade. Spread mushroom sauce over. Roll up and cut into eight. Serve with potatoes, mushrooms and carrots. Garnish with watercress and oyster mushrooms.

TIME: *preparation 20 minutes; cooking 13 minutes*
NUTRIENTS PER SERVING: *Calories 360; Total fat 25 g; Fibre 0.5 g; Carbohydrate 12 g*

FOOD EDITOR'S TIP

It is important to remove the paper from the roulade while it's still hot.

Pancake cones

- 8 oz (225 g) plain flour
- 1 teaspoon salt
- 2 eggs (size 3), beaten
- 15 fl oz (426 ml) semi-skimmed milk
- 4 teaspoons vegetable oil
- 1 onion, chopped
- 2 garlic cloves, crushed
- 8 oz (225 g) spinach, washed and trimmed
- 4 oz (100 g) frozen sweetcorn
- 15¼ oz (432 g) can red kidney beans, drained
- 1 teaspoon ground nutmeg
- 7 oz (200 g) vegetarian cheddar, grated

1 Sift flour and salt into a bowl, make a well in centre. Mix together eggs and milk. Gradually pour into flour, beating until smooth.
2 Heat ½ teaspoon oil in an 8 inch (20.5 cm) frying pan. Coat base of pan with batter. Cook for 3 minutes until edges curl up. Flip pancake, cook for a further 3 minutes. Slide on to greaseproof paper.
3 Repeat step 2 to make eight pancakes in total. Stack between greaseproof paper.
4 Dry-fry onion and garlic in a nonstick pan for 3 minutes. Add spinach, sweetcorn and beans. Cook for 5 minutes. Add nutmeg and seasoning.
5 Put filling into centre of each pancake. Sprinkle over all but 3 oz (75 g) cheddar. Roll pancakes into cones, put in greased 3 pint (1.7 litre) ovenproof dish. Top with remaining cheddar and cook at 400°F (200°C), Gas 6 for 20 minutes until golden.
6 Serve with tomato sauce, cabbage with fennel seeds, and carrots. Garnish with parsley.

TIME: *preparation 25 minutes; cooking 1 hour 16 minutes*
NUTRIENTS PER SERVING: *Calories 650; Total fat 32 g; Fibre 5 g; Carbohydrate 62 g*

Cheese puffs

- 1 lb (450 g) potatoes, roughly chopped
- 1 oz (25 g) butter, melted
- 1 teaspoon black pepper
- 1 teaspoon dijon mustard
- 1 small bunch spring onions, chopped
- 6 oz (150 g) vegetarian cheddar, cubed
- 1 lb 2oz (500 g) packet frozen puff pastry, thawed
- 1 egg (size 3), beaten

1 Cook potatoes in salted boiling water for 15 minutes or until tender. Drain. Mash with butter, black pepper and mustard. Stir in spring onions and cheese. Set aside and keep warm.
2 Roll out pastry on a lightly floured surface to ¼ inch (6 mm) thickness. Using a saucer, cut out four 6 inch (15 cm) circles. Using a smaller saucer, mark centre to give ½ inch (1.3 cm) rim.
3 Put pastry rounds on wetted baking sheets. Spoon potato mixture on to centre of each pastry circle. Knock up pastry edges with a knife. Brush pastry rim with egg. Cook at 425°F (220°C), Gas 7 for 15 minutes.
4 Serve with grilled tomatoes and peas. Garnish with lemon wedges and fresh dill.

TIME *preparation 15 minutes; cooking 30 minutes*
NUTRIENTS PER SERVING: *Calories 680; Total fat 44 g; Fibre 2 g; Carbohydrate 55 g*

FOOD EDITOR'S TIP

If potatoes are still very wet when drained, return to clean pan and put over a high heat for a minute to dry out. Continue as for recipe.

Spicy piperade

- 6 tablespoons olive oil
- 4 slices soft grain bread
- 1 onion, sliced
- 1 each red, yellow and green pepper, deseeded and finely sliced
- 8 oz (225 g) tomatoes, blanched and peeled
- 2 tablespoons chopped fresh parsley
- 1 small red chilli, deseeded and finely chopped
- 1 oz (25 g) butter
- 8 eggs (size 3), beaten
- pinch of cayenne pepper

1 Heat 1½ tablespoons oil in a frying pan. Cook one slice of bread for 1 minute each side, drain. Repeat with remaining bread, drain. Keep hot.
2 Add onion and peppers to pan. Cook for 5 minutes, stirring continuously. Add tomatoes, parsley and chilli, cover and cook for 5 minutes.
3 Meanwhile, melt butter in a nonstick pan. Pour in eggs, season with salt and cayenne pepper, stir continuously until just scrambled.
4 Halve bread and top with egg and pepper mixture. Serve with baked potatoes. Garnish with parsley.

TIME: *preparation 15 minutes; cooking 18 minutes*
NUTRIENTS PER SERVING: *Calories 560; Total fat 40 g; Fibre 4 g; Carbohydrate 31 g*

FOOD EDITOR'S TIP

The seeds of the chilli are the hottest part. If you really like spicy food you can leave the seeds in the recipe.

Tomato fusilli bake

- 1 medium aubergine, thinly sliced
- 1 oz (25 g) salt
- 8 oz (225 g) fusilli pasta shapes
- 2 leeks, sliced
- 3 garlic cloves, crushed
- 5 oz (125 g) Greek strained yogurt
- 8 oz (225 g) vegetarian cheddar, grated
- 1 oz (25 g) pine nut kernels
- 1 oz (25 g) fresh soft grain breadcrumbs
- 3 tomatoes, sliced

1 Sprinkle aubergine with salt. Stand for 30 minutes. Meanwhile, cook pasta in salted boiling water for 12 minutes. Drain.
2 Dry-fry leeks and garlic in a nonstick pan for 5 minutes. Remove from heat. Stir in yogurt.
3 Mix together cheese, pine kernels and breadcrumbs. Season
4 Rinse, drain and pat dry aubergines. Cube all but eight slices. Layer cubed aubergine, leeks, pasta and all but 2 oz (50 g) cheddar in a 3 pint (1.7 litre) ovenproof dish. Layer remaining aubergine slices on top. Cook at 350°F (180°C), Gas 4 for 50 minutes. Serve with mixed salad and peppers.

TIME: *preparation 25 minutes; standing 30 minutes; cooking 1 hour 7 minutes*
NUTRIENTS PER SERVING: *Calories: 560; Total fat 29 g; Fibre 7 g; Carbohydrate 59 g*

FOOD EDITOR'S TIP

Don't worry about excess moisture from the aubergines; the breadcrumbs will absorb this during cooking.

Rhogan-style veggies

- 1 lb (450 g) potatoes, parboiled
- 4 tablespoons vegetable oil
- 1 onion, sliced
- 2 garlic cloves, crushed
- 2 teaspoons cumin seeds
- 1 tablespoon Madras curry powder
- 1 teaspoon ground turmeric
- 2 teaspoons ground coriander
- 8 oz (225 g) French beans
- 8 oz (225 g) ripe tomatoes, quartered
- 1 green pepper, deseeded and sliced
- 5 oz (125 g) Greek strained yogurt

1. Cut potatoes into bite-sized pieces. Set aside. Heat oil in a nonstick saucepan. Add onion, garlic, cumin seeds, curry powder, turmeric and coriander, and cook for 5 minutes.
2. Stir in potatoes, French beans, tomatoes and pepper. Stir, cover and simmer for 20 minutes or until tender. Stir in yogurt.
3. Serve with rice, poppadoms, chopped cucumber and tomatoes, and chutney. Garnish with lemon wedges, chopped parsley and red-skinned onion.

TIME: *preparation 17 minutes; cooking 25 minutes*
NUTRIENTS PER SERVING: *Calories 260; Total fat 15 g; Fibre 4 g; Carbohydrate 28 g*

FOOD EDITOR'S TIP

To parboil potatoes cook in salted boiling water for about 10-12 minutes. Be careful not to overcook.

Wild mushroom cups

- 2 oz (50 g) butter, melted
- 4 large sheets filo pastry
- 2 tablespoons sesame oil
- 2 garlic cloves, crushed
- ½ inch (1.3 cm) piece fresh root ginger, peeled and finely chopped
- 1 onion, finely chopped
- 4 oz (100 g) cep mushrooms
- 4 oz (100 g) oyster mushrooms, chopped
- 4 oz (100 g) shiitake mushrooms, quartered
- 4 oz (100 g) fresh spinach, chopped
- 1 teaspoon sesame seeds
- 1 oz (25 g) walnuts

1. Put four ramekin dishes upside down on two baking sheets, well spaced apart. Brush with butter. Quarter each filo pastry sheet.
2. Brush one pastry quarter with butter. Lay over dish with ends flat on baking sheet.
3. Repeat step 2 with the other quarters to make a star. Repeat steps 2 and 3 to make four stars.
4. Cook on middle shelf at 350°F (180°C), Gas 4 for 30 minutes. Five minutes before end of cooking time, heat oil in frying pan or wok. Fry garlic, ginger and onion for 5 minutes.
5. Stir-fry all mushrooms for 5 minutes. Add spinach and sesame seeds, fry for 3 minutes. Lift cases off dishes. Fill with mushroom mixture.
6. Top with nuts. Garnish with spring onions. Serve with ratatouille and sautéd potatoes.

TIME: *preparation 25 minutes; cooking 38 minutes*
NUTRIENTS PER SERVING: *Calories 325; Total fat 21 g; Fibre 2 g; Carbohydrate 29 g*

FOOD EDITOR'S TIP

If it is easier, use a selection of English mushrooms such as button, chestnut or flat.

Vegetable croquettes

- 1½ lb (675 g) potatoes, diced
- 4 tablespoons milk
- 2 oz (50 g) frozen petit pois, thawed
- 2 oz (50 g) frozen sweetcorn, thawed
- 1 red pepper, deseeded and chopped
- 4 oz (100 g) vegetarian edam, cubed
- 2 oz (50 g) plain flour
- 2 eggs (size 3), beaten
- 7 oz (200 g) fresh breadcrumbs
- corn oil for shallow frying

1 Boil the potatoes in lightly salted water for 15 minutes. Drain, mash with milk and season.
2 Add peas, sweetcorn, pepper and edam. Cool.
3 When cold, divide mixture into eight equal portions. Shape into 4 inch (10 cm) rounds. Put on to a baking sheet and chill for 15 minutes.
4 Dip each croquette in flour, then beaten egg, then breadcrumbs. Chill again for 10 minutes.
5 Fry croquettes in oil in two batches for 5 minutes each side. Drain on kitchen paper.
6 Serve with grilled tomatoes and peas. Garnish with lemon, lime and fresh chives.

TIME: *preparation 35 minutes; chilling 25 minutes; cooking 35 minutes*
NUTRIENTS PER SERVING: *Calories 500; Total fat 18 g; Fibre 4 g; Carbohydrate 70 g*

FOOD EDITOR'S TIP

The croquettes can be shaped into fingers, if preferred.

Vegetable lasagne

- 2 tablespoons vegetable oil
- 1 onion, roughly chopped
- 2 garlic cloves, crushed
- 2 lb (900 g) mixed seasonal vegetables
- 14 oz (397 g) can chopped tomatoes
- 2 tablespoons tomato purée
- 2 oz (50 g) butter
- 2 oz (50 g) plain flour
- 1 pint (568 ml) skimmed milk
- 5 oz (125 g) vegetarian cheddar, grated
- 8 oz (225 g) packet no-cook lasagne

1 Heat vegetable oil in a large frying pan and fry chopped onion and garlic for 3 minutes until softened.
2 Wash vegetables, peel if necessary, and dice. Add to pan and fry for 5 minutes, stirring. Stir in chopped tomatoes and tomato purée. Simmer for 10 minutes until thickened.
3 Meanwhile, to make sauce, melt butter in a large saucepan. Stir in plain flour and cook for 1 minute, stirring continuously. Gradually add milk, bring to boil, stirring until thickened. Remove pan from heat. Stir in 3 oz (75 g) cheese.
4 Layer cooked vegetables, lasagne sheets and cheese sauce alternately in a 3 pint (1.7 litre) greased ovenproof dish, finishing with a layer of cheese sauce. Sprinkle over remaining grated cheese and cook at 375°F (190°C), Gas 5 for 30 minutes until lasagne is bubbling and golden. Serve with mixed green salad leaves and hot garlic bread.

TIME: *preparation 30 minutes; cooking 48 minutes*
NUTRIENTS PER SERVING: *Calories 670; Total fat 30 g; Fibre 9 g; Carbohydrate 77 g*

FOOD EDITOR'S TIP

Use a wok to cook the vegetables if your pan isn't big enough.

Herby hotpot

- 1 large onion, sliced
- 1 garlic clove, crushed
- 4 sticks celery, washed and sliced
- 4 courgettes, trimmed and sliced
- 6 carrots, peeled and thickly sliced
- 4 small turnips, trimmed
- 12 patty pan squash
- 2 tablespoons olive oil
- 2 tablespoons plain flour
- 15 fl oz (426 ml) vegetable stock
- 1 teaspoon vegetable extract
- 2 tablespoons tomato purée
- 2 lb (900 g) baking potatoes, sliced
- 2 teaspoons traditional herb mustard

1 Fry onion and garlic with all vegetables except baking potatoes in olive oil for 10 minutes, or until just tender. Remove from pan with a slotted spoon and reserve.
2 Add flour to pan and cook for 1 minute. Remove from heat and stir in stock, vegetable extract and tomato purée. Cook over a medium heat until thickened and smooth. Stir in reserved vegetables.
3 Place in a 2½ pint (1.4 litre) ovenproof dish. Arrange a double layer of sliced potato on top to cover completely.
4 Cover with oiled foil and cook at 375°F (190°C), Gas 5 for 35 minutes. Remove foil and brush potatoes with mustard. Cook for 25 minutes or until potatoes are tender and golden.
5 Garnish with sage and chives.

TIME: *preparation 30 minutes; cooking 1 hour 11 minutes*
NUTRIENTS PER SERVING: *Calories 330; Total fat 8 g; Fibre 9 g; Carbohydrate 58 g*

FOOD EDITOR'S TIP

If patty pan squash are unavailable use an extra 4 courgettes.

Spicy bean burgers

- 8 oz (225 g) country bean mixture
- 2 large onions
- 2 garlic cloves, crushed
- 1 inch (2.5 cm) piece root ginger, peeled and grated
- 2 tablespoons mild curry paste
- 1 tablespoon corn oil
- 1 egg (size 3)
- 2 tablespoons chopped coriander leaves
- 4 sesame seed baps, halved
- 2 tomatoes, sliced
- few lollo biondo lettuce leaves
- 1 small avocado, sliced

1 Put beans into a bowl and cover with boiling water. Leave to soak for 2 hours. Drain and put into a large saucepan. Cover with cold water. Bring to the boil, boil rapidly, uncovered, for 10 minutes. Reduce heat, cover pan and simmer for 45 minutes or until tender. Drain. Rinse well with cold water.
2 Chop one onion. Put in food processor with garlic, ginger, curry paste, corn oil, egg and coriander leaves. Blend until finely chopped. Spoon into a large bowl.
3 Put cooked beans into food processor and blend until just smooth. Add to bowl and mix to combine all of the ingredients well. Season with salt.
4 Divide into four and shape into 4 inch (10 cm) burgers. Put on a baking sheet and chill for 15 minutes. Cook at 400°F (200°C), Gas 6 for 20 minutes or until tender, turning halfway through cooking time.
5 Meanwhile, toast baps and slice remaining onion. Arrange lettuce on base of each. Top with burger, tomato, avocado and onion. Season with pepper. Serve with fries and relish.

TIME: *preparation 30 minutes; soaking 2 hours; chilling 15 minutes; cooking 1¼ hours*
NUTRIENTS PER SERVING: *Calories 400; Total fat 13 g; Fibre 10 g; Carbohydrate 58 g*

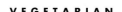

Spinach tart

- 12½ oz (340 g) packet frozen puff pastry, thawed
- 8 oz (225 g) spinach
- 1 yellow pepper, deseeded and sliced
- 6 tomatoes, cut into wedges
- 2 garlic cloves, finely sliced
- 10½ oz (285 g) jar condiverdi, drained
- 12 sun-dried tomatoes in oil, drained

1 Roll out pastry on a lightly floured surface. Using a saucer as a template cut out four rounds. Using a sharp knife, score a circle ½ inch (1.3 cm) in from rim. Put pastry on baking sheet spaced apart.
2 Dampen rims with water and prick centres with a fork. Chill for 30 minutes. Cook at 400°F (200°C), Gas 6 for 15 minutes.
3 Remove from oven. Reduce heat to 375°F (190°C), Gas 5. Arrange spinach, yellow pepper, tomatoes, garlic, condiverdi and sun-dried tomatoes in layers in pastry case. Season each layer well. Cook in oven for 15 minutes. Serve with mixed salad.

TIME: *preparation 40 minutes; chilling 30 minutes; cooking 30 minutes*
NUTRIENTS PER SERVING: *Calories 610; Total fat 46 g; Fibre 3 g; Carbohydrate 44 g*

FOOD EDITOR'S TIP

If pastry rounds don't fit on one baking sheet, you could use an upturned roasting tin.

Greek kebabs

- 4 oz (100 g) bulgar wheat
- 2 onions
- 1 lb (450 g) assorted mushrooms, such as chestnut, shiitake, button, finely chopped
- 2 garlic cloves, crushed
- 2 oz (50 g) pine nuts
- pinch each of ground cinnamon, nutmeg and allspice
- 2 tablespoons freshly chopped mint
- 1 oz (25 g) butter, melted
- 2 lemons
- 3 tablespoons olive oil
- ¼ white cabbage, shredded
- cucumber, halved and sliced
- 6 tomatoes, cut into thin wedges
- 2 tablespoons fresh coriander
- 2 tablespoons fresh parsley
- 4 pitta breads
- 12 black olives
- 2 tablespoons olive oil
- 1 teaspoon coriander seeds
- 1 red chilli deseeded and finely chopped

1 Soak bulgar in cold water for 10 minutes, drain and pat dry with clean tea towel. Meanwhile, finely chop one onion. Mix bulgar together with chopped onion, mushrooms, garlic, pine nuts, spices and mint. Season well. Pour on melted butter and bind mixture together.
2 Chill for 10 minutes, shape into mini patties, chill for further 10 minutes. Meanwhile, cut one lemon into wedges. Grill with patties for 15 minutes, turning regularly until browned.
3 Slice remaining onion. Squeeze juice from remaining lemon and whisk with olive oil. Stir in sliced onion, cabbage, cucumber, tomatoes, coriander and parsley. Season well.
4 Toast pitta breads and split open. Fill with salad, bulgar patties, grilled lemon, black olives. Sprinkle with coriander seeds and chillies and garnish with coriander.

TIME: *soaking 10 minutes; preparation 15 minutes; chilling 20 minutes; cooking 15 minutes*
NUTRIENTS PER SERVING: *Calories 460; Total fat 15 g; Fibre 4 g; Carbohydrate 68 g*

Cheesy potato rosti

- 2 lb (900 g) baking potatoes, grated (not rinsed)
- 1 red-skinned onion, grated
- 1 packet fresh chives
- 4 oz (100 g) emmenthal
- 6 tablespoons corn oil
- 20 cherry tomatoes
- 8 shiitake mushrooms
- 4 eggs (size 3)

1 Mix together unrinsed grated potato with onion, chives, cheese and seasoning. Divide mixture into four.

2 Heat 2 tablespoons oil in a small nonstick frying pan. Spoon half rosti into pan and press down with the back of a spoon. Fry for 3-5 minutes, turn and cook for 5 more minutes. Remove from pan and keep hot.

3 Repeat with remaining rosti mixture. Put tomatoes and mushrooms in a grill pan, drizzle with remaining oil and grill for 5 minutes until softened. Fry eggs. Cut each rosti into two and top with an egg. Serve with grilled tomatoes and mushrooms and French bread.

TIME: *preparation 10 minutes; cooking 25 minutes*
NUTRIENTS PER SERVING: *Calories 390; Total fat 15 g; Fibre 4 g; Carbohydrate 46 g*

FOOD EDITOR'S TIP

It is important not to rinse the starch out of the potatoes as this helps keep the rosti together.

Courgette brioche

- 1 brioche plait, sliced horizontally into 4
- 4 tablespoons olive oil
- 1 each large red and yellow pepper, deseeded and sliced into sticks
- 4 garlic cloves, roughly chopped
- 4 courgettes, rinsed and trimmed
- 3 eggs (size 3)
- 2 tablespoons freshly chopped chervil
- 2 tablespoons freshly chopped tarragon
- 7 fl oz (200 ml) carton crème fraîche

1 Line four individual gratin dishes with the brioche slices. Drizzle over oil. Put peppers and garlic in bowl. Using a vegetable peeler slice thin ribbons of carrot and courgette.

2 Gently mix all vegetables together and divide between gratin dishes. Lightly beat together eggs, herbs, crème fraîche and seasoning. Pour over vegetables, dividing equally between dishes.

3 Cook at 375°F (190°C), Gas 5 for about 15 minutes until brioche is golden and egg mixture has set.

4 Serve with French-style peas and garnish with basil.

TIME: *preparation 15 minutes; cooking 15 minutes*
NUTRIENTS PER SERVING: *Calories 520; Total fat 26 g; Fibre 5 g; Carbohydrate 58 g*

FOOD EDITOR'S TIP

Served on its own, this makes a perfect dinner party starter.

HALE AND HEARTY

Stuffed pancakes

- 8 oz (225 g) wholemeal plain flour, sifted
- 2 eggs (size 3), beaten
- 1 pint (568 ml) skimmed milk
- 4 tablespoons vegetable oil
- 2 red peppers, deseeded and sliced
- 8 oz (225 g) cooked chicken
- 4 oz (100 g) canned sweetcorn
- 10 fl oz (284 ml) white sauce
- 2 oz (50 g) gruyère, grated

1 Put flour in bowl. Beat in eggs and milk. Season.
2 Heat a little oil in a frying pan over a medium heat. Pour 5 tablespoons batter in pan and cook pancake for 1 minute, flip over and cook for a further 1 minute.
3 Repeat step 2 to make eight pancakes. Put greaseproof paper between each. Keep hot.
4 Fry red pepper in remaining oil for 2 minutes. Add chicken and corn.
5 Divide the chicken mixture between pancakes and roll up. Put into a shallow 3 pint (1.7 litre) oven dish.
6 Pour over white sauce. Sprinkle with gruyère. Grill for 5 minutes.
7 Serve pancakes with stir-fried vegetables, garnished with fresh coriander.

TIME: *preparation 25 minutes; cooking 30 minutes.*
NUTRIENTS PER SERVING: *Calories 690; Total fat 35 g; Fibre 7 g; Carbohydrate 59 g*

Chargrilled chicken burgers

- 4 chicken quarters, skinned
- 3 tablespoons sunflower oil
- 3 oz (75 g) fresh breadcrumbs
- 1 teaspoon hot chilli powder
- 1 teaspoon ground mixed spice
- 1 teaspoon ground cumin
- 1 egg (size 3), beaten
- 4 sesame seed buns
- 4 tablespoons mayonnaise
- 2 tomatoes, sliced
- 1 baby gem lettuce
- 8 tablespoons sweetcorn relish

1 Put chicken in a roasting tin, brush with oil and cook for 45 minutes. To test the chicken is done, prick with a skewer, the juices should run clear.
2 Slice into burger-sized chunks. Mix breadcrumbs with chilli powder, mixed spice and cumin. Season. Coat chicken pieces in egg and then breadcrumb mixture.
3 Grill for 15 minutes, turning once.
4 Split sesame buns and toast open sides. Spread buns with mayonnaise, fill with tomatoes, lettuce leaves, 1 tablespoon sweetcorn relish and chicken pieces. Serve with baked potatoes and the remaining lettuce leaves, tomato slices and sweetcorn relish.

TIME *preparation 20 minutes; cooking 1 hour*
NUTRIENTS PER SERVING: *Calories 495; Total fat 22 g; Fibre 0 g; Carbohydrate 46 g*

FOOD EDITOR'S TIP

If you can't cut chicken in one large piece, serve three or four small pieces in each bun.

Open chicken pie

- 8 oz (225 g) ready-made wholemeal pastry
- 1 egg (size 3), beaten
- 2 leeks, washed, trimmed and sliced
- 8 oz (225 g) broccoli florets
- 1 courgette, cut lengthways and thinly sliced
- 1 tablespoon sesame seeds
- 1 oz (25 g) butter
- 1 oz (25 g) plain flour
- 10 fl oz (284 ml) skimmed milk
- 1 oz (25 g) gruyère, grated
- 8 oz (225 g) frozen chicken thawed, cooked and cut into strips

1 Roll out pastry thinly and use to line an 8 inch (20 cm) greased pie dish. Trim away excess pastry.
2 Re-roll trimmings and cut out pastry leaves . Brush edge of pastry case with half the beaten egg and lay leaves around edge, overlapping slightly. Prick base. Chill for 10 minutes.
3 Meanwhile, steam leeks, broccoli florets and the courgette for 3 minutes.
4 Brush pastry case with remaining egg, sprinkle leaves with sesame seeds. Bake blind at 400°F (200°C), Gas 6 for 20 minutes.
5 Meanwhile, melt butter in a saucepan. Add flour, cook for 1 minute. Gradually stir in milk. Bring to boil, stirring, and cook for 1 minute until thickened. Remove from heat. Season well. Stir in gruyère.
6 Stir chicken and green vegetables into cheese sauce and stir over a low heat until heated through.
7 Spoon chicken filling into pastry case. Serve immediately with sweetcorn and green salad.

TIME: *preparation 25 minutes; chilling 10 minutes; cooking 23 minutes*
NUTRIENTS PER SERVING: *Calories: 490; Total fat 30 g; Fibre 6 g; Carbohydrate 33 g*

FOOD EDITOR'S TIP

This is an ideal dish for using up leftover cooked chicken.

Tangy chicken

- 6 tablespoons vegetable oil
- 1 medium onion, finely chopped
- 1 garlic clove, crushed
- 2 x 14 oz (397 g) cans chopped tomatoes with chilli spices
- 3 tablespoons tomato and chilli relish
- 2 tablespoons chopped fresh parsley, or 2 teaspoons dried
- 8 x 3 oz (75 g) chicken thighs, skinned

1 Heat 2 tablespoons oil in a large heavy-based frying pan. Add onion and garlic and cook for 3 minutes until golden and softened.
2 Stir in chopped tomatoes and relish and boil rapidly for 5 minutes until thickened. Season well. Stir in parsley.
3 Heat remaining oil in a frying pan. Add chicken and fry over a low heat for 15 minutes until golden.
4 Pour tomato sauce over. Simmer for 10 minutes.
5 Spoon chicken and sauce on to four serving plates. Serve with rice, garnished with fresh flat leaf parsley.

TIME: *preparation 15 minutes; cooking 33 minutes*
NUTRIENTS PER SERVING: *Calories 510; Total fat 43 g; Fibre 2 g; Carbohydrate 45 g*

FOOD EDITOR'S TIP

To really heat things up, stir in a small deseeded chopped chilli.

Thatched soup

- 1½ lb (675 g) frozen chicken breasts, thawed
- 1 lb (450 g) flat mushrooms, sliced
- 10 fl oz (284 ml) chicken stock
- 1 pint (568 ml) semi-skimmed milk
- 1 oz (25 g) butter
- 1 oz (25 g) plain flour
- 12 oz (350 g) frozen puff pastry, thawed

1 Remove skin and bones from chicken breasts. Put chicken, mushrooms, stock and milk into a large pan. Bring to boil, simmer for 30 minutes.
2 Remove chicken and mushrooms. Process stock and half of mushrooms until smooth.
3 Melt butter. Add flour, stir for 1 minute. Add stock. Bring to boil, stirring for 5 minutes.
4 Dice chicken, stir into soup with remaining mushrooms. Season and pour into four 10 fl oz (284 ml), 6 inch (15 cm) ovenproof soup bowls.
5 Roll out pastry to a 12 inch (30.5 cm) square. Cut out four 6 inch (15 cm) circles. Dampen edges and use to cover soup bowls.
6 Cook at 425°F (220°C), Gas 7 for 15 minutes. Serve with steamed vegetables and grated cheddar.

TIME: *preparation 25 minutes; cooking 51 minutes*
NUTRIENTS PER SERVING: *Calories 550; Total fat 34 g; Fibre 4 g; Carbohydrate 35 g*

FOOD EDITOR'S TIP

The bowls will be easier to lift out of the oven if they are placed on a baking sheet first.

Cheesy chicken rolls

- 2 x 1 lb (450 g) bags frozen part-boned chicken breasts, thawed
- 4 oz (100 g) full-fat soft cheese
- 1 garlic clove, crushed
- 1 tablespoon chopped fresh rosemary
- 5¾ oz (145 g) packet pizza base mix
- 1 egg (size 3), beaten
- 1 tablespoon sesame seeds

1 Using a sharp knife, remove chicken breasts from bone. Make an incision along one edge of each breast to form a pocket.
2 Beat together cheese, garlic and rosemary. Divide into four and spoon into each pocket.
3 Make up pizza base mix according to packet instructions. Divide dough into four and roll out each piece into a large rectangle.
4 Brush each with egg. Put chicken on top. Fold dough over and seal with egg. Put seam side down on a greased baking sheet. Brush with egg and sprinkle with sesame seeds.
5 Cook at 375°F (190°C), Gas 5 for 30 minutes. Garnish with rosemary, serve with mashed potatoes, mangetout and sweetcorn.

TIME: *preparation 25 minutes; cooking 30 minutes*
NUTRIENTS PER SERVING: *Calories 440; Total fat 23 g; Fibre 1 g; Carbohydrate 25 g*

FOOD EDITOR'S TIP

This is a cheat's way of turning a dish into an *en croûte* and very effective, too.

Countryside chicken

- 2 tablespoons vegetable oil
- 4 x 8 oz (225 g) chicken quarters
- 2 medium onions, thinly sliced
- 8 oz (225 g) carrots, thickly sliced
- 8 oz (225 g) swede, diced
- 6 oz (150 g) button mushrooms, halved
- 1 tablespoon milk
- 1 tablespoon sesame seeds
- 15 fl oz (426 ml) chicken stock
- 2 tablespoons cornflour

1 Heat oil in a 3 pint (1.7 litre) flameproof casserole dish. Fry chicken for 5 minutes, turning once, until golden then remove with a slotted spoon.
2 Add onions, carrots and swede to pan. Cook for 5 minutes or until just tender. Add mushrooms and return chicken to pan.
3 Pour stock over chicken. Cover and cook at 350°F (180°C), Gas 4, stirring occasionally for 1 hour until tender.
4 Remove chicken pieces with a slotted spoon and keep hot on serving plates. Blend cornflour with a little water to form a smooth paste. Add to casserole and stir over a low heat for 2 minutes until thickened.
5 Spoon sauce and vegetables over chicken quarters. Garnish with thyme and serve with hot rolls and steamed courgettes.

TIME: *preparation 22 minutes; cooking 1 hour 12 minutes*
NUTRIENTS PER SERVING: *Calories 360; Total fat 16 g; Fibre 4 g; Carbohydrate 22 g*

FOOD EDITOR'S TIP

Look out for part-baked rolls at your supermarket. They come in various types and can be cooked and served hot with the chicken.

Drumstick risotto

- 3 oz (75 g) butter
- 1 tablespoon vegetable oil
- 8 x 4 oz (100 g) chicken drumsticks
- 1 onion, finely chopped
- 4 oz (100 g) celery sticks, chopped
- 8 oz (225 g) carrots, finely chopped
- 4 fl oz (114 ml) dry white wine
- 12 oz (325 g) arborio rice
- 1½ pints (852 ml) chicken stock
- 4 oz (100 g) frozen garden peas
- 1 tablespoon chopped fresh parsley

1 Melt butter with oil in a large frying pan. Add drumsticks and cook for 15 minutes, turning, until golden. Remove from pan. Set aside.

2 Put onion, celery and carrots in pan and cook for 2-3 minutes. Stir in white wine and cook for 3 minutes, or until liquid has reduced slightly.

3 Stir in rice and stock. Return drumsticks to pan. Bring to boil and simmer for 20 minutes, or until stock is absorbed and rice is tender.

4 Stir in peas and parsley, cook for a further 10 minutes until chicken is cooked. Season. Serve garnished with lemon wedges and parsley.

TIME: *preparation 20 minutes; cooking 51 minutes*
NUTRIENTS PER SERVING: *Calories 730; Total fat 27 g; Fibre 4 g; Carbohydrate 81 g*

FOOD EDITOR'S TIP

For young children it's easier if you bone the drumsticks first and cut into bite-sized pieces.

Chicken nuggets and chips

- 4 x 6 oz (150 g) boneless, skinless chicken breasts
- 1 egg (size 3), beaten
- 6 oz (150 g) medium oatmeal
- 1 oz (25 g) parmesan, grated
- 1 teaspoon chilli powder
- 2 lb (900 g) potatoes, unpeeled and parboiled
- sunflower oil for deep-fat frying

1 Cut chicken into bite-sized chunks. Put egg in one small bowl, and oats, parmesan and chilli in another, season well.

2 Dip chicken pieces in egg then oat mixture, coating thoroughly. Chill chicken for 15 minutes.

3 Meanwhile, cut parboiled potatoes into chips. Heat oil to 375°F (190°C). Deep-fry chips in two batches for 5 minutes each. Drain on kitchen paper, set aside.

4 Deep-fry chicken nuggets in two batches, for 5 minutes each. Drain and keep hot. Re-fry chips in two batches for 5 minutes each until crisp. Drain on kitchen paper. Garnish with flat leaf parsley and serve with a selection of relishes.

TIME: *preparation 20 minutes; chilling 15 minutes; cooking 30 minutes*
NUTRIENTS PER SERVING: *Calories 600; Total fat 26 g; Fibre 3 g; Carbohydrate 51 g*

FOOD EDITOR'S TIP

Only dip the chicken pieces lightly in the egg so there is enough to coat all of them.

Bacon drumsticks with honey sauce

- 8 oz (225 g) smoked streaky bacon, derinded
- 8 x 4 oz (100 g) chicken drumsticks
- 3 tablespoons clear honey
- 1 tablespoon light soy sauce

1 Stretch bacon with the back of a knife until doubled in length. Wrap a rasher of bacon around each drumstick and secure with a cocktail stick.

2 Put honey and soy sauce in a saucepan and warm gently. Put chicken drumsticks on an oiled baking sheet and brush with honey sauce.

3 Cook at 350°F (180°C), Gas 4 for 30-35 minutes or until the juices run clear when a chicken drumstick is pierced with a skewer.

4 Remove cocktail sticks from drumsticks and serve with chips and baked beans.

TIME: *preparation 12 minutes; cooking 35 minutes*
NUTRIENTS PER SERVING: *Calories 275; Total fat 14 g; Fibre 0 g; Carbohydrate 9 g*

FOOD EDITOR'S TIP

These bacon drumsticks are equally delicious eaten cold.

Crunchy chicken salad

- 1 lb (450 g) boneless, skinless chicken breasts
- 1 tablespoon lemon juice
- 1 tablespoon sesame seeds
- 15 oz (425 g) can red kidney beans, rinsed and drained
- 2 oranges, peeled and segmented
- 4 oz (100 g) button mushrooms, sliced
- 3 spring onions, finely chopped
- 1 yellow pepper, halved, deseeded and cut into strips
- 3 oz (75 g) walnut halves
- 6 oz (150 g) spinach

Dressing:
- 5 oz (125 g) carton natural yogurt
- 1 tablespoon lemon juice
- ¼ teaspoon paprika

1 Toss chicken breasts in lemon juice. Sprinkle with sesame seeds.

2 Cook under hot grill for 15 minutes until tender, turning halfway through cooking time. Cut into bite-sized chunks.

3 Toss in a bowl with remaining salad ingredients. Season. Spoon into individual serving bowls.

4 Mix together dressing ingredients, season, and drizzle over salad just before serving.

TIME: *preparation 35 minutes; cooking 15 minutes*
NUTRIENTS PER SERVING: *Calories 400; Total fat 18 g; Fibre 9 g; Carbohydrate 28 g*

FOOD EDITOR'S TIP

Watch chicken carefully when grilling so as not to burn sesame seeds.

Fluffy savoury omelette

- 4 oz (100 g) smoked streaky bacon, derinded
- 10 fl oz (284 ml) white sauce
- 2 fl oz (57 ml) single cream
- 4 chicken drumsticks, cooked
- 4 oz (100 g) button mushrooms, halved
- 8 eggs (size 3), separated
- 2 tablespoons vegetable oil

1. Cook bacon under a preheated grill for 5 minutes until crisp and golden, turning once. Roughly chop.
2. Put white sauce and single cream in a pan and stir over a low heat until smooth.
3. Remove meat from drumsticks. Discard bones and skin. Cut into bite-sized pieces and stir into sauce with bacon and mushrooms. Bring to boil, stirring, and cook for 3 minutes.
4. Lightly beat egg yolks. Whisk egg whites until stiff peaks form and fold into beaten yolks.
5. Heat ½ tablespoon oil in an 8 inch (20 cm) omelette pan. Spoon in one-quarter of the omelette mixture and cook over a medium heat for 3-4 minutes, until set and underside is golden brown. Keep hot. Repeat with remaining mixture to make four omelettes in total.
6. Put on serving plates. Fill with hot chicken mixture. Serve with baked potatoes and salad.

TIME: *preparation 25 minutes; cooking 24 minutes*
NUTRIENTS PER SERVING: *Calories 470; Total fat 34 g; Fibre Trace; Carbohydrate 9 g*

FOOD EDITOR'S TIP

If you prefer, make one giant omelette and then cut it into four.

Turkey pilaf

- 4 oz (100 g) frozen chopped spinach
- 2 tablespoons sunflower oil
- 1 onion, chopped
- 5½ oz (135 g) packet mixed brown and wild rice
- ½ teaspoon ground cinnamon
- 12 fl oz (341 ml) chicken stock
- 2 oz (50 g) no-need-to-soak dried apricots, quartered
- 1 oz (25 g) raisins
- 1 lb (450 g) cooked turkey, chopped
- 1 oz (25 g) cashew nuts, roughly chopped
- 10 oz (275 g) cooked weight basmati rice

1. Put spinach in a saucepan and stir over a low heat for about 4 minutes or until thawed. Cover and cook for 2 minutes. Leave to cool.
2. Heat oil in a heavy-based pan. Add chopped onion and cook gently for 3-4 minutes until softened. Stir in mixed brown and wild rice, spinach, cinnamon and seasoning.
3. Add chicken stock to pan. Bring to boil. Reduce heat, cover and cook for 15 minutes.
4. Add apricots, raisins and cooked turkey, but don't stir in. Cover and cook for 20 minutes.
5. Add nuts and basmati rice. Stir on low heat for 1 minute. Garnish with fresh coriander.

TIME: *preparation 15 minutes; cooking 42 minutes*
NUTRIENTS PER SERVING: *Calories 490; Total fat 15 g; Fibre 7 g; Carbohydrate 52 g*

FOOD EDITOR'S TIP

Ask for a piece of cooked turkey at the delicatessen counter so you can cut it into chunks.

Turkey patties

- 1 lb (450 g) minced turkey
- 2 oz (50 g) fresh white breadcrumbs
- 1 egg (size 3), beaten
- 1 teaspoon English mustard powder
- 1 tablespoon dried mixed herbs
- 2 cloves garlic, crushed
- ½ small onion, finely chopped
- 4 oz (100 g) mature cheddar

1 Put all the ingredients, except the cheddar into a large bowl and mix well. Season well.

2 Turn out on to a lightly floured surface and knead lightly. Divide into four. Pat each piece in to a 6 inch (15 cm) round. Cut cheese into four even slices. Lay a slice in the centre of each round. Pull meat up around the cheese. Pinch and seal to form cutlets.

3 Put cutlets seam-side down on a wire rack over a grill pan. Grill under a medium heat for 10 minutes each side until golden. Serve with sautéd potatoes and mushrooms, grilled tomatoes, fried egg and baked beans. Garnish with flat leaf parsley.

TIME: *preparation 10 minutes; cooking 20 minutes*
NUTRIENTS PER SERVING: *Calories 275; Total fat 12 g; Fibre 0 g; Carbohydrate 7 g*

FOOD EDITOR'S TIP

Ring the changes by using different mince, seasoning and cheese.

Cheesy thatched pies

- 1 medium onion, finely chopped
- 1½ lb (675 g) minced beef
- 8 oz (225 g) carrots, diced
- 2 tablespoons plain flour
- 12 fl oz (341 ml) beef stock
- 2 tablespoons tomato purée
- 2 tablespoons Worcestershire sauce
- 2 teaspoons dried mixed herbs
- 2 oz (50 g) frozen sweetcorn
- 2 oz (50 g) frozen peas
- 6 oz (150 g) instant mashed potato pieces
- 2 tablespoons mayonnaise
- 1 oz (25 g) butter
- 2 oz (50 g) cheddar, grated

1 Dry-fry onion in a large nonstick frying pan for 3 minutes. Add mince and cook for 10 minutes, stirring occasionally, until browned.

2 Stir carrots and flour into the mince and cook for 1 minute. Pour in stock and bring to boil. Stir well.

3 Add purée, Worcestershire sauce, herbs, sweetcorn and peas, and simmer for 20 minutes until thickened, stirring occasionally.

4 Meanwhile, make up mashed potato, according to instructions. Stir in mayonnaise and butter and beat potato mixture until smooth.

5 Divide meat mixture between four 10 fl oz (284 ml) pie dishes. Cover with mashed potato and fluff up using a fork.

6 Sprinkle grated cheddar over top and cook at 375°F (190°C), Gas 5 for 15 minutes or until golden. Serve the pies with fresh mixed salad leaves and tomato wedges.

TIME: *preparation 15 minutes; cooking 49 minutes.*
NUTRIENTS PER SERVING: *Calories 550; Total fat 24 g; Fibre 5 g; Carbohydrate 42 g*

FOOD EDITOR'S TIP

These pies can be made in advance and reheated in the microwave on Full Power.

Sloppy joes

- 2 medium onions
- 1½ lb (675 g) minced beef
- 1 tablespoon vegetable oil
- 2 green peppers, roughly chopped
- 2 teaspoons mild chilli powder
- 1 teaspoon plain flour
- 10 fl oz (284 ml) beef stock
- 2 tablespoons Worcestershire sauce
- 4 wholemeal pitta breads
- 8 oz (225 g) tomatoes, thinly sliced
- ¼ cucumber, thinly sliced
- 1 little gem lettuce

1 Finely chop 1 onion and dry-fry in nonstick frying pan for 3 minutes. Add mince and cook for 10 minutes, stirring occasionally, until browned. Remove.
2 Heat oil. Slice remaining onion and stir-fry with green pepper for 4 minutes until softened. Stir in chilli powder and plain flour. Cook for 1 minute, stirring continuously.
3 Add stock and Worcestershire sauce. Bring to boil. Stir in cooked mince and simmer for 10 minutes until thickened, stirring occasionally.
4 Meanwhile, grill pitta breads for 4 minutes, turning once. Halve and split open to form pockets.
5 Fill with meat, tomato, cucumber and lettuce. Serve garnished with lemon wedges and spring onions.

TIME: *preparation 30 minutes; cooking 28 minutes*
NUTRIENTS PER SERVING: *Calories 440; Total fat 12 g; Fibre 5 g; Carbohydrate 42 g*

FOOD EDITOR'S TIP

As an alternative, use the filling in baked potatoes.

Two layer lasagne

- 1½ oz (40 g) butter
- 1 tablespoon vegetable oil
- 8 oz (225 g) onions, sliced
- 12 oz (325 g) leeks, trimmed and sliced
- 14 oz (397 g) can chopped tomatoes
- 12 oz (325 g) courgettes, sliced
- 1 teaspoon garlic purée
- 2 tablespoons tomato purée
- 1 lb (450 g) lean minced beef
- 1 oz (25 g) plain flour
- 10 fl oz (284 ml) skimmed milk
- 4 oz (100 g) red leicester, grated
- 8 sheets no-cook lasagne verdi

1 Heat ½ oz (15 g) butter and vegetable oil in a large heavy-based saucepan. Add onion and leeks and cook over a low heat for 4 minutes or until softened, stirring occasionally.
2 Stir in chopped tomatoes and courgettes with ½ teaspoon garlic purée and 1 tablespoon tomato purée. Cover and simmer for 30 minutes, stirring occasionally.
3 Meanwhile dry-fry mince in a nonstick pan for 10 minutes until browned. Stir in remaining tomato and garlic purées. Cook for 2 minutes. Set aside.
4 Melt remaining butter in a saucepan. Stir in flour and cook for 1 minute, stirring. Remove from heat and gradually stir in milk. Stir over a low heat until thickened. Season. Stir in half grated cheese.
5 Lightly oil a 3 pint (1.7 litre) ovenproof dish. Spoon half the meat mixture into base. Cover with half of ratatouille then four sheets of lasagne. Repeat layering with remaining ingredients, finishing with a layer of cheese sauce.
6 Sprinkle over the remaining cheese and cook at 375°F (190°C), Gas 5 for 40 minutes or until top is bubbling and golden.
7 Serve with a green leaf salad.

TIME: *preparation 40 minutes; cooking 1 hour 27 minutes*
NUTRIENTS PER SERVING: *Calories 720; Total fat 47 g; Fibre 6 g; Carbohydrate 41 g*

Chilli tacos

- 1 lb (450 g) lean minced beef
- 2 onions, finely chopped
- 1½ oz (39 g) packet taco seasoning mix
- 1 tablespoon tomato purée
- 15¼ oz (432 g) can red kidney beans, drained
- 2 avocados
- 2 garlic cloves, crushed
- 1 lime, juice only
- 8½ oz (235 g) jar hot taco sauce
- 12 taco shells
- 5 fl oz (142 ml) fresh soured cream
- pinch of paprika

1 Cook mince in a nonstick frying pan for 4-5 minutes or until brown. Add onions and cook for 3 minutes until tender. Drain off excess fat.

2 Stir in taco seasoning, tomato purée, 6 fl oz (170 ml) water and kidney beans. Bring to boil. Simmer for 20 minutes or until thickened.

3 Meanwhile, halve avocados, remove stone and peel and chop flesh. Put in a blender or food processor with garlic, lime juice and half the jar of taco sauce. Blend for 2 minutes until smooth.

4 Fill taco shells with beef mixture. Put on a baking sheet and cook at 350°F (180°C), Gas 4 for 5 minutes to heat through. Spoon soured cream over each taco and sprinkle with paprika. Serve with avocado mixture, remaining taco sauce, grated cheddar, diced red pepper and mixed salad leaves.

TIME: *preparation 30 minutes; cooking 33 minutes*
NUTRIENTS PER SERVING: *Calories 730; Total fat 47 g; Fibre 4 g; Carbohydrate 38 g*

FOOD EDITOR'S TIP

It is easier to fill the taco shells if you first stand them in a small deep-sided dish.

Cheese haggerty

- 3 tablespoons vegetable oil
- 1 onion, finely chopped
- 1 garlic clove, crushed
- 1 lb (450 g) lean minced beef
- 2 tablespoons tomato purée
- 2 lb (900 g) large potatoes
- 4 oz (100 g) cheddar
- 10 fl oz (284 ml) beef stock
- 1 oz (25 g) melted butter
- 1 tablespoon chopped fresh parsley

1 Heat 1 tablespoon oil in a large frying pan. Cook onion and garlic for 3-4 minutes until soft and golden.

2 Add mince, cook for 5-6 minutes. Stir in tomato purée and cook for a further 1 minute. Remove from pan and set aside. Clean pan.

3 Thinly slice potatoes. Brush pan with remaining oil. Spread half potatoes over base, season and sprinkle with half cheese.

4 Spoon over mince. Pack down with back of a spoon. Sprinkle with remaining cheese. Arrange remaining potatoes over top.

5 Pour in stock. Cover with a tight-fitting lid and cook over a low heat for 40 minutes. Uncover and cook for a further 5 minutes.

6 Brush potatoes with melted butter and grill until golden.

TIME: *preparation 25 minutes; cooking 56 minutes*
NUTRIENTS PER SERVING: *Calories 640; Total fat 35 g; Fibre 7 g; Carbohydrate 50 g*

FOOD EDITOR'S TIP

Make sure you cook over a low heat or the potatoes at the bottom of the pan will burn.

Corned beef hash

- 2 lb (450 g) potatoes
- 2 tablespoons sunflower oil
- ½ oz (15 g) butter
- 8 oz (225 g) onions, thinly sliced
- 1 red pepper, thinly sliced
- 2 x 12 oz (325 g) cans corned beef, cubed
- ½ savoy cabbage, finely shredded

1   Put potatoes in a large pan of salted water and bring to the boil. Simmer for 10-12 minutes. Drain.
2   Roughly chop potatoes. Heat oil and butter in a large nonstick frying pan until melted. Add potatoes and stir-fry for 10 minutes, mashing potato gently so it starts to break up.
3   Add onions and peppers and stir-fry for 5 minutes until potato is golden. Add cabbage and corned beef and stir-fry for 5 minutes or until beef is golden and warmed through. Season well and serve immediately.

TIME: *preparation 20 minutes; cooking 32 minutes*
NUTRIENTS PER SERVING: *Calories 580; Total fat 31 g; Fibre 4 g; Carbohydrate 26 g*

FOOD EDITOR'S TIP

You might have an attachment on your food processor for shredding cabbage which makes life easier.

Sausage pinwheels and jackets

- 4 baking potatoes
- 2 lb (900 g) string herb and pork sausages
- 2 red-skinned onions
- 1 tablespoon sunflower oil
- 15½ oz (435 g) can tomato soup
- 2 teaspoons wholegrain mustard
- 3 tablespoons red wine vinegar
- 2 tablespoons brown sugar
- 2 spring onions, chopped
- 1 oz (25 g) butter, melted
- 2 oz (50 g) Greek strained yogurt

1   Thread potatoes on to skewers and cook at 400°F (200°C), Gas 6 for 1½ hours until tender.
2   Meanwhile, untwist sausages and ease sausagemeat together to form one long sausage.
3   Measure sausage into four equal lengths, carefully twist and snip to form four long sausages.
4   Coil each sausage into a pinwheel and push a skewer through the centre to secure.
5   Grill or barbecue pinwheels for 20 minutes turning occasionally to brown evenly. Meanwhile, chop one onion and slice the other into rings. Brush onion rings with oil and cook for 15 minutes with the sausages, until soft.
6   Put chopped onion in saucepan with tomato soup, mustard, vinegar, sugar and 1 tablespoon chopped spring onion. Simmer for 10 minutes.
7   Halve baked potatoes, scoop out flesh and mash with butter and yogurt. Season. Refill potato skins, sprinkle with remaining chopped spring onion. Serve with sausages, onion rings and tomato sauce. Garnish with parsley.

TIME: *preparation 25 minutes; cooking 1½ hours*
NUTRIENTS PER SERVING: *Calories 930; Total fat 62 g; fibre 3 g; Carbohydrates 65 g*

FOOD EDITOR'S TIP

Try using chipolata sausages for bite-sized pinwheels.

Herby sausage ratatouille

- ¼ oz (7.5 g) butter
- 1 tablespoon vegetable oil
- 8 oz (225 g) onions, sliced
- 12 oz (325 g) leeks, trimmed and sliced
- 14 oz (397 g) can chopped tomatoes
- 12 oz (325 g) courgettes, sliced diagonally
- ½ teaspoon garlic purée
- 1 tablespoon tomato purée
- 1 lb (450 g) lincolnshire sausages

1 Heat butter and vegetable oil in a large heavy-based frying pan. Add sliced onion and leeks and cook over a low heat for 4 minutes or until softened, stirring occasionally.
2 Stir in chopped tomatoes and sliced courgettes with garlic and tomato purées. Cover and simmer ratatouille for 30 minutes, stirring occasionally.
3 Meanwhile, grill sausages for 10 minutes, turning frequently, until golden. Cut sausages in half diagonally.
4 Stir sausage pieces into ratatouille and reheat for 2 minutes.
5 Spoon on to hot serving plates and garnish with a sprig of fresh flat leaf parsley. Serve with basmati rice, garnished with toasted flaked almonds.

TIME: *preparation 25 minutes; cooking 36 minutes*
NUTRIENTS PER SERVING: *Calories 480; Total fat 37 g; Fibre 4 g; Carbohydrate 21 g*

FOOD EDITOR'S TIP

Try making double the quantity and freeeze for another day.

Sausage and bacon bean pie

- 2 lb (900 g) potatoes, cut into pieces
- 2 garlic cloves, peeled
- 1 onion, sliced
- 2 fl oz (57 ml) olive oil
- 1 lb (450 g) smoked bacon joint, cubed into bite-sized pieces
- 1 lb (450 g) pork and beef sausages
- 14 oz (397 g) can chopped tomatoes with fennel
- 15¼ oz (432 g) can red kidney beans, drained

1 Put potatoes and garlic cloves in a pan and cover with cold water. Cover and bring to boil. Reduce heat and simmer for 20 minutes or until potatoes are tender.
2 Meanwhile, fry onion in 2 tablespoons olive oil until soft. Add bacon and sausages and fry until golden. Remove sausages from pan, leave to cool slightly and cut each sausage diagonally into three pieces.
3 Return sausages to pan, add tomatoes with fennel and kidney beans. Simmer for 15 minutes or until tender.
4 Drain potatoes and garlic. Mash together until smooth or blend in food processor, gradually adding remaining olive oil and plenty of seasoning.
5 Spoon sausage mixture into a 3 pint (1.7 litre) flameproof dish. Spoon over potato mixture to cover completely. Cook under a preheated grill for 5 minutes or until top is golden. Serve accompanied by steamed sliced courgettes and diced carrots.

TIME: *preparation 20 minutes; cooking 25 minutes*
NUTRIENTS PER SERVING: *Calories 980; Total fat 60 g; Fibre 6 g; Carbohydrate 68 g*

FOOD EDITOR'S TIP

If you can't find canned tomatoes with fennel, use ordinary chopped tomatoes and add ¼ teaspoon dried mixed herbs.

Pork casserole

- 1½ lb (675 g) pork sausages
- 1 lb (450 g) carrots, peeled and quartered
- 8 oz (225 g) baby turnips
- 1 tablespoon vegetable oil
- 2 onions, thinly sliced
- 1 oz (25 g) plain flour
- 2 teaspoons tomato purée
- 1 orange, grated rind and juice
- 15 fl oz (426 ml) pork stock
- 1 tablespoon chopped fresh parsley

1 Halve the sausages. Cut carrots into sticks. Peel turnips and cut into wedges.
2 Heat oil in a casserole dish. Cook sausages for 10 minutes, turning, until browned. Remove from dish and set aside.
3 Add onions to casserole, cook for 3-4 minutes. Stir in flour, purée and rind, cook for 1 minute.
4 Add sausages, carrots and turnips to casserole. Stir in orange juice and stock. Bring to boil, stirring, until thickened. Cover, simmer for 1 hour, or until vegetables are tender.
5 Remove from heat. Season, stir in parsley. Garnish with parsley, serve with crusty bread.

TIME: *preparation 25 minutes; cooking 1¼ hours*
NUTRIENTS PER SERVING: *Calories 720; Total fat 58 g; Fibre 4 g; Carbohydrate 31 g*

FOOD EDITOR'S TIP

If liked, replace baby turnips with a swede cut into bite-sized pieces.

Sausage goulash

- 1 lb (450 g) beef and pork sausages
- 2 onions, sliced
- 1 tablespoon plain flour
- 1 tablespoon paprika
- 1 tablespoon tomato purée
- 14 oz (397 g) can chopped tomatoes
- 10 fl oz (284 ml) beef stock
- 14 oz (397 g) can pimientos, drained
- 11 oz (300 g) can button mushrooms, drained

1 Using a sharp knife, cut sausages in half. Heat a nonstick frying pan. Dry-fry sausages for 5 minutes, turning occasionally, until lightly browned on all sides. Remove from frying pan with a slotted spoon and set aside.
2 Add onions to frying pan and cook for 3 minutes, or until soft and lightly browned. Stir in flour and paprika and cook for 1 minute, stirring continuously.
3 Stir in tomato purée, chopped tomatoes and beef stock. Add reserved sausages. Slowly bring mixture to boil. Cover and simmer gently for 25 minutes.
4 Roughly chop pimientos. Add to goulash with button mushrooms and seasoning. Cook for a further 10 minutes or until tender.
5 Garnish goulash with chopped parsley and serve with Granary bread and butter.

TIME: *preparation 25 minutes; cooking 44 minutes*
NUTRIENTS PER SERVING: *Calories 548; Total fat 17 g; Fibre 14 g; Carbohydrate 96 g*

FOOD EDITOR'S TIP

For a really spicy flavour, use a can of chopped tomatoes with chilli seasoning; and for an extra filling meal serve brown rice with the goulash.

Apricot pork

- 1 oz (25 g) butter
- 1 bunch spring onions, chopped
- 4 oz (100 g) fresh breadcrumbs
- 3 oz (75 g) ready-to-eat dried apricots, chopped
- 1 egg (size 3)
- 4 x 6 oz (150 g) boneless pork loin chops
- 4 tablespoons apricot chutney

1 Mix together butter, spring onions, breadcrumbs, apricots and egg. Make a deep slit in side of pork chops to form a pocket. Fill each pocket with apricot stuffing. Chill for 15 minutes.

2 Brush chops with apricot chutney. Grill for 25 minutes, turning once.

3 Serve chops with carrots, broccoli and gravy.

TIME: *preparation 15 minutes; chilling 15 minutes; cooking 25 minutes*
NUTRIENTS PER SERVING: *Calories 310; Total fat 14 g; Fibre 2 g; Carbohydrate 21 g*

FOOD EDITOR'S TIP

If you have any stuffing left over, make individual patties and grill with the pork.

Lincolnshire toady

- 4 oz (100 g) plain flour, sifted
- ¼ teaspoon salt
- 1 egg (size 3)
- 5 fl oz (142 ml) skimmed milk
- 5 fl oz (142 ml) cold water
- 3 tablespoons sunflower oil
- 1 lb (450 g) lincolnshire sausages
- 4 oz (100 g) onions, thickly sliced
- 4 oz (100 g) button mushrooms, halved

1 Put flour and salt into a large bowl and make a well in centre. Add egg and milk and beat until smooth. Gradually stir in cold water. Set aside.

2 Preheat oven to 425°F (220°C), Gas 7. Pour 2 tablespoons oil into two 8 inch (20.5 cm) cake tins. Put in oven for 5 minutes or until oil is sizzling.

3 Grill sausages for 5 minutes, turning occasionally until lightly browned. Meanwhile cook onions and mushrooms in remaining oil for 5 minutes.

4 Put half the sausages, onions and mushrooms into each tin. Divide batter between tins pouring it around the sausages and vegetables. Cook for 30-35 minutes until well risen and golden brown.

5 Serve with gravy, boiled potatoes, baked carrots and sautéd courgettes. Garnish potatoes with chopped flat leaf parsley.

TIME: *preparation 15 minutes; cooking 45 minutes*
NUTRIENTS PER SERVING: *Calories 600; Total fat 46 g; Fibre 1 g; Carbohydrate 34 g*

FOOD EDITOR'S TIP

Make sure the oil is really sizzling hot before you pour in the sausages and the batter.

Ribs with spicy potatoes

- 2 lb (900 g) pork spare ribs
- 7 oz (200 g) jar smoky barbecue sauce
- 1 garlic clove, crushed
- 2 tablespoons soft dark brown sugar
- 1 tablespoon dark soy sauce
- 1 teaspoon olive oil
- 1 lb (450 g) new potatoes
- 1 green chilli, sliced
- ½ small red pepper, deseeded and diced
- 1 teaspoon dried chilli flakes
- 1 teaspoon coarse sea salt

1   Trim excess fat from ribs and put ribs into a large bowl. Mix together the barbecue sauce, garlic, sugar, soy sauce and oil. Pour over ribs and coat each thoroughly. Leave to marinate.
2   Meanwhile, cut out four 9 inch (23 cm) squares of foil. Divide potatoes equally between each and top with a little green chilli, red pepper, chilli flakes and sea salt.
3   Gather edges of each foil square together to form a parcel and twist to seal. Put parcels on to a baking sheet and cook at 400°F (200°C), Gas 6 for 1 hour.
4   Remove ribs from marinade and arrange, spaced slightly apart, on a rack set over a roasting tin. Brush marinade over then cook on top shelf for a further 30 minutes, or until ribs and potatoes are tender.
5   Put ribs on to serving plates with potatoes in opened foil parcels, steamed green beans and baked crispy coated onion rings.

TIME: *preparation 25 minutes; cooking 1½ hours*
NUTRIENTS PER SERVING: *Calories 600; Total fat 39 g; Fibre 1 g; Carbohydrate 45 g*

FOOD EDITOR'S TIP

If you have time marinate the ribs overnight for even more flavour.

Spinach and apple pie

- ½ oz (15 g) butter, melted
- 8 oz (225 g) cooking apples
- 1 tablespoon soft dark brown sugar
- 1 lb (450 g) rindless back bacon
- 1 lb (450 g) potatoes, parboiled
- 12 oz (325 g) frozen chopped spinach, thawed
- 1 teaspoon ground nutmeg
- 5 fl oz (142 ml) chicken stock
- 12 oz (325 g) frozen puff pastry, thawed
- 1 egg (size 3), beaten

1   Brush base and sides of a 3½ pint (2 litre) ovenproof dish with melted butter. Peel and core apples and cut into ¼ inch (6 mm) slices. Put in base of dish, overlapping slightly. Sprinkle over sugar.
2   Cut bacon into strips. Scatter over apple slices. Cut parboiled potatoes into ¼ inch (6 mm) slices. Arrange on top of bacon.
3   Squeeze spinach between two plates to extract excess water. Put into a bowl and season well. Stir in nutmeg. Spoon over potatoes. Pour over chicken stock.
4   Roll out pastry a little larger than dish on a surface lightly dusted with flour. Brush edge of dish with a little beaten egg and lay pastry over filling. Press edges to rim and trim to neaten edges.
5   Mark surface of pastry with a sharp knife and knock up edges. Brush lid with remaining egg. Cook pie at 350°F (180°C), Gas 4 for 45 minutes, or until pastry is golden. Serve with sweetcorn, sliced carrots and garnish with green salad leaves.

TIME: *preparation 40 minutes; cooking 45 minutes*
NUTRIENTS PER SERVING: *Calories 900; Total fat 67 g, Fibre 4 g; Carbohydrate 55 g*

FOOD EDITOR'S TIP

Grilling the bacon first before using in the pie gives a more crispy result.

Cheese and ham calzone

- 14 oz (397 g) can chopped tomatoes with herbs
- 2 tablespoons tomato purée
- 1 green pepper, deseeded and diced
- 10½ oz (290 g) packet pizza base mix
- 4 oz (100 g) smoked ham, sliced wafer-thin
- 4 oz (100 g) feta or edam cheese, diced
- 1 egg (size 3), beaten

1. Put chopped tomatoes, tomato purée and pepper in a saucepan and bring to the boil. Simmer for 8 minutes until very thick.
2. Make up pizza base mix according to packet instructions. Divide into four and roll out each to a 9 inch (23 cm) circle. Put on two greased baking sheets spaced a little apart.
3. Spread tomato sauce over each pizza circle, spreading to within 1 inch (2.5 cm) of edge. Scatter over ham and feta cheese. Brush dough with beaten egg and fold circles in half. Twist edges to seal. Glaze and cook at 425°F (220°C), Gas 7 for 15 minutes. Serve with mixed salad.

TIME: *preparation 25 minutes; cooking 23 minutes*
NUTRIENTS PER SERVING: *Calories 400; Total fat 11 g; Fibre 2 g; Carbohydrate 55 g*

FOOD EDITOR'S TIP

Don't be over generous when spreading the tomato sauce or it will 'leak'.

Gammon bean bake

- 2 tablespoons sunflower oil
- 1 onion, finely sliced
- 2 garlic cloves, crushed
- 15¼ oz (432 g) can chilli beans in chilli sauce
- 15¼ oz (432 g) can borlotti beans, drained
- 3 tablespoons Worcestershire sauce
- 3 tablespoons tomato purée
- 1 oz (25 g) soft light brown sugar
- 10 fl oz (284 ml) vegetable stock
- 8 oz (225 g) tendersweet gammon steaks, cubed
- 1 lb (450 g) swede, thinly sliced
- 2 oz (50 g) mature cheddar, grated

1. Heat oil in a saucepan and cook onion and garlic for 5-6 minutes until golden. Add beans, Worcestershire sauce, tomato purée, sugar and stock. Cook until sugar dissolves.
2. Add gammon, simmer for 15 minutes, stirring.
3. Meanwhile, boil swede for 5 minutes. Drain.
4. Spoon gammon mixture into four 10 fl oz (284 ml) ovenproof dishes. Arrange swede over top.
5. Sprinkle with cheese. Cook at 375°F (190°C), Gas 5 for 20 minutes. Serve with steamed broccoli, mangetout and yellow pepper.

TIME: *preparation 20 minutes; cooking 41 minutes*
NUTRIENTS PER SERVING: *Calories 400; Total fat 15 g; Fibre 22 g; Carbohydrate 38 g*

FOOD EDITOR'S TIP

Replace the gammon with button mushrooms and the cheddar with a vegetarian cheese for a vegetarian version of this dish.

Sticky ribs with sweetcorn rice

- 6 tablespoons vegetable oil
- 3 tablespoons demerara sugar
- 2 tablespoons tomato ketchup
- 2 lb (900 g) lamb riblets
- 1 medium onion, finely chopped
- 1 garlic clove, crushed
- 2 x 14 oz (397 g) cans chopped tomatoes, with chilli spices
- 4 tablespoons barbecue sauce
- 1½ lb (675 g) cooked rice
- 4 oz (100 g) frozen sweetcorn
- 4 oz (100 g) green beans, sliced into 1 inch (2.5 cm) lengths

1   Mix together 2 tablespoons each oil and demerara sugar with ketchup in a small pan until melted. Brush over riblets and cook under a preheated grill for 12 minutes, basting and turning.
2   Meanwhile, beat 2 tablespoons oil in a large heavy-based frying pan. Add onion and garlic and cook for 3 minutes until golden. Stir in chopped tomatoes and boil rapidly for 5 minutes until thickened. Season.
3   Stir in remaining demerara sugar and barbecue sauce. Bring to boil and simmer for 10 minutes, stirring occasionally.
4   Heat remaining oil. Stir-fry rice, sweetcorn and beans for 5 minutes. Season well. Keep hot.
5   Sieve tomato sauce. Spoon sauce and rice into separate serving bowls. Garnish rice with toasted flaked almonds. Put riblets on serving plate. Garnish with sprigs of fresh watercress.

TIME: *preparation 15 minutes; cooking 17 minutes*
NUTRIENTS PER SERVING: *Calories 765; Total fat 39 g; Fibre 4 g; Carbohydrate 89 g*

Don't worry if ribs blacken a little at the edges – it adds to the flavour.

Tomato and liver pot

- 1 oz (25 g) plain flour, seasoned
- 1½ lb (675 g) lambs' liver, thinly sliced
- 1½ oz (40 g) butter
- 1 lb (450 g) onions, thinly sliced
- 5 fl oz (142 ml) vegetable stock
- 10 fl oz (284 ml) skimmed milk
- 2 tablespoons dry sherry
- 3 tablespoons tomato purée
- ¼ teaspoon garlic purée
- 2 tablespoons chopped fresh parsley

1   Put flour and sliced liver in a polybag and shake well until liver is evenly coated.
2   Melt butter in a large frying pan. Add liver and cook for 5 minutes, turning occasionally, until browned. Remove with a slotted spoon.
3   Fry onions in pan for 5 minutes until softened. Gradually stir in stock, milk, sherry and tomato and garlic purées with 1 tablespoon chopped fresh parsley. Bring to the boil, stirring continuously.
4   Return liver to pan. Cover and continue to cook over a gentle heat for 15 minutes.
5   Spoon liver on to hot serving plates. Sprinkle with remaining parsley before serving wih tagliatelle.

TIME: *preparation 20 minutes; cooking 25 minutes*
NUTRIENTS PER SERVING: *Calories 430; Total fat 25 g; Fibre Trace; Carbohydrate 13 g*

You may be able to find frozen, ready-sliced lambs' liver at the supermarket. Thaw completely before using.

Lamb with apricots and couscous

- 12 oz (325 g) couscous
- 1 pint (568 ml) warm water
- 1½ lb (675 g) middle neck lamb
- 4 oz (100 g) butter
- 8 oz (225 g) pickling onions
- 1 garlic clove, crushed
- 8 oz (225 g) carrots, halved and quartered
- 1 tablespoon tomato purée
- 14 oz (397 g) can chopped tomatoes
- 10 fl oz (284 ml) lamb stock
- 3 oz (75 g) no-need-to-soak apricots

1 Soak couscous in warm water in a large bowl for 30 minutes.
2 Cut lamb into 1 inch (2.5 cm) cubes, removing any excess fat. Melt 2 oz (50 g) butter in large saucepan. Add onions, garlic and carrots and cook for 3-4 minutes.
3 Add lamb to pan and cook for 5-6 minutes or until browned, stirring continuously.
4 Add tomato purée, chopped tomatoes and lamb stock to pan and bring to boil, stirring continuously. Cover pan and simmer gently for 20 minutes.
5 Stir in apricots. Drain couscous in heat-proof colander. Put colander over the lamb stew and cover. Cook for 40 minutes. Remove from heat, stir remaining butter into couscous. Serve garnished with chopped fresh parsley.

TIME: *preparation 25 minutes; soaking 30 minutes; cooking 1 hour 10 minutes*
NUTRIENTS PER SERVING: *Calories 700; Total fat 35 g; Fibre 8 g; Carbohydrate 58 g*

FOOD EDITOR'S TIP

If you can't get pickling onions use small onions, quartered, instead.

Ratatouille chops

- 13½ (390 g) can ratatouille
- 2 teaspoons tomato purée
- 8 fl oz (227 ml) vegetable stock
- ½ teaspoon dried mixed herbs
- 2 garlic cloves, crushed
- 3 tablespoons vegetable oil
- 1½ lb (675 g) bag frozen lamb loin chops, thawed

1 Put ratatouille in a saucepan. Stir in tomato purée, stock and mixed herbs. Cook over a low heat for 15 minutes until vegetables are very soft. Remove from heat and leave to cool slightly. Put into a processor and blend for 1 minute until smooth.
2 Mix garlic with oil. Put chops on rack in grill pan and brush with half of garlic oil. Cook under a preheated grill for 7-8 minutes.
3 Turn chops over and brush with remaining oil. Cook for a further 7-8 minutes or until tender.
4 Reheat sauce and spoon over lamb chops. Garnish with mint and serve with boiled potatoes, broccoli and carrots.

TIME: *preparation 20 minutes; cooking 31 minutes*
NUTRIENTS PER SERVING: *Calories 660; Total fat 56 g; Fibre 2 g; Carbohydrate 5 g*

FOOD EDITOR'S TIP

This sauce would also be delicious served with any cooked white fish.

Texan grill and chips

- 4 x 3 oz (75 g) lamb chops
- 4 lambs' kidneys, halved, skinned and cored
- 4 pork and herb sausages
- 1 each red, green and yellow pepper, deseeded and sliced
- 7 oz (198 g) jar barbecue tomato relish
- 1 tablespoon sunflower oil
- 2 lb (900 g) bag frozen oven chips

1 Trim lamb chops and put on to grill tray with kidneys, sausages and peppers.
2 Mix 3 tablespoons barbecue relish with 1 tablespoon water and use to brush chops, kidneys and sausages; brush peppers with oil. Cook under a preheated grill for 10 minutes, turning once. Remove kidneys and keep hot.
3 Turn chops and sausages and brush again with relish. Cook for 5-10 minutes.
4 Meanwhile, cook chips at 425°F (220°C), Gas 7 for 20 minutes or until golden. Garnish mixed grill with fresh watercress and serve accompanied with remaining barbecue relish.

TIME: *preparation 15 minutes; cooking 20 minutes*
NUTRIENTS PER SERVING: *Calories 800; Total fat 37 g; Fibre 6 g; Carbohydrate 89 g*

FOOD EDITOR'S TIP

Use a sharp pair of scissors to remove cores from the kidneys.

Lamb jackets

- 4 x 8 oz (225 g) baking potatoes, washed
- 1 lb (450 g) minced lamb
- 1 onion, finely chopped
- 1 garlic clove, crushed
- 14 oz (397 g) can chopped tomatoes
- 1 teaspoon English mustard
- 1 lb (450 g) can baked beans
- 7 oz (200 g) can red kidney beans, drained
- 1 teaspoon Worcestershire sauce
- 1 tablespoon soft dark brown sugar

1 Cut a cross in each potato. Cook at 350°F (180°C), Gas 4 for 1¼ hours or until tender.
2 Meanwhile, dry-fry mince in a nonstick frying pan for 5-6 minutes, stirring, until browned. Add onion and garlic and cook for 2-3 minutes.
3 Stir in tomatoes and mustard, cook for 1 minute. Add remaining ingredients. Bring to boil, cover and simmer for 20 minutes. Uncover and cook for a further 10 minutes, or until mince is tender.
4 Put potatoes on serving plates. Split, season and divide lamb mixture between each. Garnish with chopped parsley and serve with salad, tomatoes and green beans.

TIME: *preparation 15 minutes; cooking 1¼ hours*
NUTRIENTS PER SERVING: *Calories 520; Total fat 11 g; Fibre 10 g; Carbohydrate 72 g*

FOOD EDITOR'S TIP

You can also use the lamb sauce as a base for shepherd's pie.

Lamb chilli loaf

- 1½ lb (675 g) minced lamb
- 1 onion, chopped
- 1 garlic clove, crushed
- 2 teaspoons chilli seasoning
- 14 oz (397) can chopped tomatoes
- 4 tablespoons tomato purée
- 2 oz (50 g) button mushrooms
- 2 oz (50 g) canned red kidney beans, drained
- 8 oz (225 g) fresh breadcrumbs
- 14 oz (397 g) can pimientos, drained

1. Dry-fry mince for 5 minutes. Add onion and garlic, fry for a further 5 minutes. Stir in chilli seasoning, tomatoes, purée, mushrooms and beans.
2. Season and simmer uncovered for 15 minutes. Remove from heat and stir in breadcrumbs.
3. Spoon one-third of mince mixture into a greased 2 lb (900 g) loaf tin. Spread half the pimientos over. Continue to layer up using all the ingredients.
4. Cover tin with foil, put in a roasting tin half-filled with water. Cook at 350°F (180°C), Gas 4 for 1 hour. Uncover, cook for a further 45 minutes.
5. Serve with soured cream and salad leaves.

TIME: *preparation 15 minutes; cooking 2 hours 10 minutes*
NUTRIENTS PER SERVING: *Calories 490; Total fat 17 g; Fibre 5 g; Carbohydrate 44 g*

FOOD EDITOR'S TIP

Don't store remaining kidney beans in the can in the fridge. Put into a polybox and use within two or three days.

Country cottage pie

- 2 lb (900 g) potatoes
- 3 tablespoons milk
- ½ oz (15 g) butter
- 1 egg (size 3), separated
- 1 lb (450 g) minced lamb
- 1 bunch spring onions, trimmed and sliced
- 8 oz (225 g) button mushrooms, wiped
- 2 tablespoons plain flour
- 10 fl oz (284 ml) lamb stock
- 1 tablespoon Worcestershire sauce
- 1 tablespoon tomato purée
- 2 tablespoons chopped fresh parsley
- ½ teaspoon sesame seeds

1. Bring potatoes to boil in lightly salted water and cook for 15-20 minutes until tender. Drain and mash well with milk and butter. Beat in egg yolk and seasoning. Set aside.
2. Meanwhile, dry-fry mince over a medium heat until browned. Add spring onions and mushrooms. Cook for 5 minutes. Add flour, cook for 1 minute. Remove from heat and stir in stock, Worcestershire sauce and tomato purée.
3. Bring to boil, stirring continuously. Season and stir in chopped parsley. Spoon mixture into four 15 fl oz (426 ml) ovenproof dishes.
4. Whisk egg white in a clean bowl until soft peaks form. Fold into mashed potato and spoon over mince mixture.
5. Sprinkle sesame seeds over. Cook at 375°F (190°C), Gas 5 for 30 minutes or until topping is golden. Serve with grilled fresh plum tomatoes and peas, garnished with fresh parsley.

TIME: *preparation 35 minutes; cooking 50 minutes*
NUTRIENTS PER SERVING: *Calories 440; Total fat 16 g; Fibre 4 g; Carbohydrate 44 g*

FOOD EDITOR'S TIP

If liked, grate 1 oz (25 g) cheddar over the top after cooking and grill for 2 minutes.

Moussaka

- 2 large onions, chopped
- 1 garlic clove, crushed
- 14 oz (397 g) can tomatoes
- 1½ tablespoons tomato purée
- ½ tablespoon paprika
- 1½ lb (675 g) lean minced lamb
- 2 tablespoons fresh mixed herbs
- 5 fl oz (142 ml) lamb stock
- 2 aubergines, thickly sliced
- 2 oz (50 g) salt
- 2 tablespoons cornflour
- 1 pint (568 ml) skimmed milk
- 6 oz (150 g) edam, grated

1 To make tomato sauce, dry-fry one onion and the garlic for 5 minutes in a nonstick pan. Add tomatoes, purée and paprika. Cook for 20 minutes.
2 Meanwhile, in another pan, dry-fry remaining onion and the mince for 10 minutes, season well. Drain excess fat. Stir in tomato sauce and herbs. Pour lamb stock into meat mixture. Bring to boil and stir well. Simmer for 30 minutes.
3 Meanwhile, sprinkle sliced aubergines with salt, leave for 15 minutes. Rinse well, pat dry.
4 Grill aubergines for 5 minutes on both sides. Remove meat mixture from heat, season well.
5 Mix cornflour with 3 tablespoons milk. Bring rest of milk to boil. Pour cornflour mixture into hot milk. Cook, stirring, for 5 minutes until thickened. Stir in all but 3 tablespoons cheese.
6 Layer aubergines and meat mixture alternately into a 3 pint (1.7 litre) ovenproof dish finishing with a layer of aubergines.
7 Pour cheese sauce over top. Sprinkle with remaining cheese. Cook at 350°F (180°C), Gas 4 for 40 minutes or until top is golden.

TIME: *preparation 20 minutes; cooking 1¼ hours*
NUTRIENTS PER SERVING: *Calories 500; Total fat 25 g; Fibre 6 g; Carbohydrate 19 g*

Crispy pizza with salad

- 1 medium onion, chopped
- 2 garlic cloves, crushed
- 2 tablespoons tomato purée
- 14 oz (397 g) can chopped tomatoes
- 2 x 5¾ oz (145 g) packets pizza base mix
- 14.1 oz (400 g) can tuna in brine, drained
- 4 oz (100 g) button mushrooms, sliced
- 4 oz (100 g) reduced-fat cheddar, grated
- 1 small bunch fresh basil, roughly shredded

Salad:
- 5 fl oz (142 ml) low-fat mayonnaise
- ½ white cabbage, finely shredded
- 2 oz (50 g) walnut halves
- ½ green pepper, deseeded and chopped
- 1 apple, sliced
- 2 sticks celery, chopped
- 2 oz (50 g) raisins

1 Dry-fry onion and garlic in a nonstick frying pan for 2 minutes. Stir in tomato purée and chopped tomatoes and simmer for 10 minutes until thickened.
2 Meanwhile, make up pizza base mix according to packet instructions. Divide dough into quarters. Roll out each quarter to an 8 inch (20 cm) circle. Put on two greased baking sheets.
3 Spoon tomatoes over bases. Put tuna and mushrooms on top. Sprinkle over grated cheese.
4 Cook pizzas at 425°F (220°C), Gas 7 for 20-25 minutes
5 Meanwhile, make the salad by tossing together all ingredients in a large bowl. Chill.
6 Sprinkle pizzas with roughly shredded basil leaves and serve immediately with salad.

TIME: *preparation 25 minutes; cooking 37 minutes*
NUTRIENTS PER SERVING: *Calories 695; Total fat 26 g; Fibre 10 g; Carbohydrate 73 g*

Wholemeal fishfingers

- 4 x 3½ oz (87.5 g) individual packets frozen cod portions, thawed
- 6 oz (150 g) wholemeal breadcrumbs
- 2 tablespoons sesame seeds
- 4 tablespoons plain flour
- 1 egg (size 3), beaten
- 6 tablespoons vegetable oil
- 2 tablespoons capers, finely chopped
- 2 baby gherkins, finely chopped
- 4 tablespoons mayonnaise

1 Cut cod portions in half lengthways. Mix crumbs and sesame seeds. Season well.
2 Put flour and beaten egg on to separate deep plates and the breadcrumbs into a polybag. Dip fishfingers in flour and then egg. Put in polybag and coat with crumbs.
3 Heat oil in large frying pan. Cook fishfingers for 6 minutes and drain them on kitchen paper. Keep hot.
4 For tartare sauce: stir capers and gherkins into mayonnaise.
5 Serve with chips or sautéd potatoes and peas. Accompany with tartare sauce and garnish with lemon wedges.

TIME: *preparation 20 minutes; cooking 45 minutes*
NUTRIENTS PER SERVING: *Calories 510; Total fat 34 g; Fibre 3 g; Carbohydrate 32 g*

FOOD EDITOR'S TIP

Remember you cannot freeze these fishfingers uncooked as the cod has already been frozen.

Nutty fish nuggets

- 1½ lb (675 g) hoki fillet, skinned
- 6 oz (150 g) white breadcrumbs
- 1 oz (25 g) mixed chopped nuts
- 3 eggs (size 3), beaten
- 4 oz (100 g) plain flour
- 1 oz (25 g) butter
- 2 teaspoons wholegrain mustard
- 15 fl oz (426 ml) semi-skimmed milk
- vegetable oil for deep frying

1 Wash fish, dry on kitchen paper. Remove any bones, cut flesh into bite-sized pieces.
2 Mix breadcrumbs and nuts, season. Pour eggs into a shallow dish. Put breadcrumb mixture and 3 oz (75 g) flour on two plates.
3 Dip fish in flour, egg, then breadcrumbs.
4 Melt butter in a pan. Stir in remaining flour. Cook for 2 minutes. Stir in mustard and milk. Bring to boil, simmer for 20 minutes, stirring.
5 Heat oil in a 4 pint (2.3 litre) heavy-based pan or deep-fat fryer to 375°F (190°C). Cook nuggets in three batches for 5 minutes each. Drain. Serve with sauce, sautéed potatoes, cherry tomatoes and peas. Garnish with lime wedges.

TIME: *preparation 30 minutes; cooking 37 minutes*
NUTRIENTS PER SERVING: *Calories 680; Total fat 38 g; Fibre 2 g; Carbohydrate 44 g*

FOOD EDITOR'S TIP

If the bread is too fresh for making breadcrumbs dry it out in a low oven for 30 minutes first.

INDEX